THE ULTIMATE GUIDE TO
VEGAN ROASTS

Feast-Worthy Recipes Everyone Will Love

Romy London

creator of RomyLondonUK.com

PAGE STREET
PUBLISHING CO.

PAGE STREET
PUBLISHING CO.

First published in 2022 by
Page Street Publishing Co.
27 Congress Street, Suite 1511
Salem, MA 01970
www.pagestreetpublishing.com

Distributed by Macmillan, sales in Canada by The Canadian Manda Group.

26   25   24   23   22   1   2   3   4   5

ISBN-13: 978-1-64567-512-9
ISBN-10: 1-64567-512-2

Library of Congress Control Number: 2021937941

Cover and book design by Molly Kate Young for Page Street Publishing Co.
Photography by Romina Callwitz
Author photo by Emma Pharaoh

Printed and bound in the United States

DEDICATION

For my grandma Helga, who always encouraged my creativity. I'm sorry I couldn't keep the promise I made at four years old and turned out to be a photographer instead of following in your footsteps at the hair salon. Your persistence and free spirit are my biggest inspirations.

For my grandad Heinz, who taught me to go after my dreams, to not wait until tomorrow and, most important, to enjoy life. You have given me more than I could ever ask for, and I am eternally grateful.

CONTENTS

INTRODUCTION

Wow, here we are! My first cookbook! I still remember how my mum used to say "one day I'll find your recipes in a book!" when I first started sharing my recipes online. It was obvious back then that she was joking. Well, mum, here we are—and isn't it ironic?!

It was a big surprise to everyone when I went vegan overnight. Growing up on the German and Dutch borders, I was used to German cuisine—surely one of the most un-vegan ones on the planet. It wasn't until May 2014 that I finally felt I didn't want to eat animal products anymore and was ready to take steps toward veganism.

I vividly remember numerous family gatherings, elaborate Sunday lunches and festive meals filled with the best comfort food one could possibly enjoy. These wonderful meals were a regular occurrence throughout my childhood, and I think that's why these feasts hold such a big place in my heart. It is no surprise that I grew up to love festive meals and fully loaded dinner tables, dished up with all the good stuff. And surprisingly, going vegan hasn't actually changed the endless flavorsome possibilities for those feasts!

Going vegan has been anything but restrictive for me. Instead of feeling like I was missing out, it expanded my culinary horizons to so many new dishes and cuisines. I realized that everything is possible on a vegan diet, and that's exactly why I'm writing this book for you—so you never have to feel like you're missing out at those festive occasions that are usually centered around a meat dish and other non-vegan foods.

What I love most about festive roasts is the variety of flavors and textures, all combined into one fantastic meal. There is often so much choice on the table that everyone can easily find something to satisfy their taste buds. At the same time, cooking a roast dinner is such a wonderful act of love: putting all your effort into each part of the meal to share with the ones you love and value. It shows true dedication, and I think it's a beautiful way to say "I care about you."

Going vegan didn't stop my love for elaborate roast meals. They were one of the first things I experimented with in the kitchen. I set about figuring out how to make the perfect vegan roast potatoes and engaged in crazy experiments to create the best vegan Yorkshire puds—a vital part of any roast meal here in the U.K.!

Throughout the years, I've shared numerous vegan (roast) recipes on both my blog (www.romylondonuk.com) and my Instagram (@romylondonuk), and I even had the chance to demonstrate my culinary skills on a TV show as the only vegan contestant: Check out *Crazy Delicious* on Netflix, if you haven't yet!

This book is the result of numerous failed and successful roast experiments and many days and nights in the kitchen. There's a lot of love going into every single one of these dishes! It includes something roast-a-licious for every palate. Whether you like a meaty texture for your mains, call yourself a tofu lover or enjoy vegetables taking the center stage of your roast meal, I got you!

If you ask me, flavorsome side dishes are just as important as the main squeeze. That's exactly why you will find lots of sidekick options in this book, from classics such as the perfect vegan roast potatoes, to some exciting combinations that will surprise you and have you wanting more. Each recipe also includes suggestions for delicious pairings, but I always encourage you to listen to your own taste buds and get creative! And let's not forget about luscious sauces to smother your roasts in. Always remember: When it comes to gravy, the limit does not exist. At least, that's my personal roast dinner motto. Welcome to the club.

In addition, I've also marked the recipes that are gluten-free or nut-free (or have the option to be), as well as those that are best prepared in advance, so you can easily identify the ones that best fit your needs. The recipes in the Seitan Showstoppers chapter (page 63) are also labeled by the technique used to make the seitan (see Getting Started with Seitan on page 156 for more information).

I feel honored to share these recipes with you. I truly hope you will enjoy these feasts just as much as I do—whether you're veg-curious, you've invited a vegan over for a delicious roast or simply enjoy getting experimental in the kitchen. You got this!

CREATING VEGAN ROASTS

When it comes to creating stomach-filling and taste bud–satisfying roasts, there are a few vital elements. For me personally, it is a combination of aromas and textures: juicy, crisp, fluffy, creamy, smooth, crunchy, runny, firm, tender. I'm convinced that the best roast dinner includes at least three flavors and three textures to give that ultimate satisfying feel.

To assemble the perfect roast meal, I usually recommend one main dish, sometimes more if you're serving more than four people or if their tastes are extremely different. Alongside the main, I recommend three to four sides and a sauce. If you're serving a big crowd, go all out and fill the feasting table with lots of options for everyone to choose from. That's what I love to do when I invite friends over for Thanksgiving or for a food-filled get-together.

If you're a beginner to vegan roasts and are in a rush to create some luscious meals for friends and family, then head to the tofu chapter (page 45) and veggie center stage chapter (page 11). If you love experimenting, trying out new ingredients and techniques and don't shy away from spending time in the kitchen, then the seitan chapter (page 63) is for you! Don't forget to cover your luscious roasts with the most delicious sauces (page 135) and showcase them alongside some amazing side dishes (page 103).

With the help of this book, you will master vegan roasts, and I've included lots of additional tips and tricks in every single recipe to inspire you. If you'd like to learn more about seitan-making techniques, don't miss the summary at the end of the book (page 156). It will help you understand how the ingredients and processes affect its flavor and texture, so you'll be well equipped to get creative with seitan yourself!

CENTER STAGE VEGGIE ROASTS

Since moving to the U.K. in 2012, I have become a huge fan of roast dinners—in case you couldn't tell! There's simply something magical about getting together with loved ones and enjoying an abundance of good food.

As a kid that always wanted to eat her veggies, I'm especially excited about this chapter! When it comes to comfort foods, believe it or not, vegetables rank highly on my list. When you know how to properly prepare them, they turn into wonderful showstoppers for the entire family.

Here you will find vegetables taking center stage in the form of delicious roasts. They'll let your favorite vegetables shine on the feasting table! You will be diving into mouthwatering Stuffed Hasselback Squash (page 22), a Wild Mushroom Loaf (page 38) full of comforting and rich flavors and stunningly colorful Mini Rainbow Wellingtons (page 34) to wow everyone around the table—just to name a few of my favorites in this chapter.

I'm showing you vegetable recipes that are anything but boring—and that you'll actually want to eat. You won't be leaving veggies off your plate any longer. Trust me!

MUSHROOM AND LENTIL WELLINGTON

A Wellington was one of the first vegan roasts I ever made, and to this day it's one of my favorite ways to serve up a delicious roast meal. Traditionally, a Wellington is made with beef that is wrapped in a flaky puff pastry and then baked. For vegan Wellingtons, there are several delicious fillings, but this mushroom and lentil combination is a personal go-to of mine. The mushrooms add a savory taste and meat-like texture. This Wellington is easy to make with a few simple techniques, and it's definitely a stunner on any festive table spread. To make this Wellington gluten-free, use a gluten-free puff pastry.

Serves 6 to 8

For the Wellington

3 cups (470 g) washed and sliced brown mushrooms

Pinch of sea salt

2 tbsp (28 g) vegan butter

1 cup (160 g) finely diced yellow onion

⅔ cup (67 g) finely diced celery

1 cup (128 g) finely diced carrot

2 tsp (10 g) crushed garlic

½ cup (125 ml) vegan white wine

2 cups (396 g) canned green lentils

½ cup (57 g) roughly chopped walnuts

2 sheets vegan puff pastry (I use Jus-Rol 14 x 9 inches [35 x 23 cm])

1 tbsp (15 ml) tamari

1 tbsp (15 ml) plant milk

Place your mushrooms in a large, dry skillet over medium-high heat and stir frequently for 2 to 3 minutes, then sprinkle in the salt. Your mushrooms will release their water, become soft and shrink. Cook for 5 to 10 minutes, or until the majority of the liquid has evaporated from the pan. Set it aside.

In a separate skillet, heat the vegan butter and add the onion, celery and carrot. Sauté them for 5 to 7 minutes, or until soft. Add the garlic and cook for 2 to 3 minutes, then deglaze the pan with the white wine. Wait 2 minutes, then add the sautéed mushrooms to the warm skillet and remove it from the heat.

Mash 1 cup (198 g) of the green lentils with the back of a fork; keep the other cup of lentils intact. Stir the lentils into the pan, then add the walnuts and allow the mixture to cool for at least 1 hour.

In the meantime, bring your puff pastry sheets to room temperature, so they can soften and become easier to unroll.

Once cooled down, spoon the mixture onto the middle of an unrolled puff pastry sheet in a log shape—or any desired shape you wish to create! Ensure the mixture is tightly packed within the pastry sheet.

Sprinkle a little water or plant milk on the pastry edges around the log, then gently place a second puff pastry sheet on top and press the edges against the bottom sheet to seal. Use a sharp knife to remove any excess pastry. Crimp the edges between your fingers or use a fork to seal them.

(continued)

MUSHROOM AND LENTIL WELLINGTON (CONTINUED)

For Serving

The Perfect Roast Potatoes (page 104)

Vegan Yorkies (page 108)

Lemon Mustard Sauce (page 143)

Use any leftover scraps of puff pastry to decorate your Wellington. You can score it or cut out little puff pastry shapes; dab them with a little plant milk to add them onto your log.

Rest the Wellington in your fridge or freezer for a minimum of 1 hour, then preheat your oven to 375°F (190°C) and place a rack in the middle. Line a baking sheet with parchment paper.

For the vegan egg wash, combine the tamari and plant milk in a small bowl. Brush it onto your Wellington. Roast the Wellington for 25 to 30 minutes, or until it is beautifully golden on the outside.

This recipe is simply divine served alongside roast potatoes, Yorkies and lemon mustard sauce—yum!

GARLIC AND THYME MUSHROOM ROAST PIE

In pies, we crust! If, like me, you're obsessed with all things pastry, then this one is for you. Luscious aromas of mushrooms, roasted garlic and fresh thyme will make every single guest drool. Wrapped in buttery puff pastry, this pie is the ultimate eye-catcher on the dinner table. And it's actually simple to make in a few easy steps—there's no reason not to try it!

I recommend using a deep, perforated pie dish to make this. The little holes in the dish ensure that your pastry bakes golden all the way around and prevents a soggy bottom. If you don't have such a dish, I recommend skipping the pastry bottom and edges and simply topping an ovenproof dish with a pastry lid and serving with a large spoon.

If you're gluten-free, don't you worry! Choose gluten-free puff pastry sheets and replace the flour in this recipe with 2 tablespoons (16 g) of cornstarch.

Serves 6 to 8

For the Pie

46 oz (1.3 kg) sliced chestnut mushrooms

3 tbsp (7 g) fresh thyme

1 tbsp (15 ml) olive oil

½ cup (111 g) finely diced yellow onion

4 tsp (18 g) crushed garlic

2 tbsp (28 g) vegan butter

4 tbsp (24 g) all-purpose flour

1 cup (240 ml) dairy-free cream

3 tbsp (45 ml) tamari, divided

¼ tsp ground black pepper

1 cup (240 ml) vegetable stock

2 sheets vegan puff pastry (I use Jus-Rol 14 x 9 inches [35 x 23 cm])

In a large, dry skillet, heat the mushrooms over medium heat. Stir regularly for 15 to 20 minutes, until they release their water. Continue to cook until the majority of the water has evaporated from the pan, then stir in the fresh thyme. Remove the mushrooms from the skillet and set them aside.

Heat the olive oil in the skillet over medium heat. Sauté the onion and garlic for 5 minutes. Add the vegan butter and as soon as it has melted, sprinkle in the all-purpose flour. Stir everything into a paste, then pour in the dairy-free cream and stir until everything is well combined.

Add 1 tablespoon (15 ml) of the tamari and black pepper. Pour in the vegetable stock and continue to stir for 5 to 10 minutes, or until the mixture thickens. Remove the skillet from the heat and stir in the cooked mushrooms, then set it aside to cool for 30 minutes.

In the meantime, grease a 9-inch (23-cm) round pie dish and sprinkle it with a little flour to prevent your pie from sticking to the dish.

Unroll 1 puff pastry sheet and carefully place it over the pie dish. Gently press it into all the edges of the dish and cut off any excess. Use a fork to pierce the bottom about eight to ten times.

(continued)

GARLIC AND THYME MUSHROOM ROAST PIE (CONTINUED)

For Serving

The Perfect Roast Potatoes
(page 104) or Ranch Potato
Mash (page 115)

Smoky Crusted Green Beans
(page 131)

Brandy Peppercorn Sauce
(page 140)

Preheat your oven to 375°F (190°C).

Add the cooled mushroom mixture to the pie dish. Unroll the second puff pastry sheet and carefully place it on top, cutting off any excess with a sharp knife. Gently seal the edges with a fork. Use any pastry leftovers to decorate the pie or use a knife to gently score it. Brush the top of the pie with the remaining tamari. Bake for 25 to 30 minutes, or until golden.

Once golden on top, remove your pie from the oven and allow it to sit for 10 minutes before carefully removing it from the pie dish. Cut it into slices and serve alongside roast potatoes or ranch potato mash, crusted green beans and brandy peppercorn sauce.

SHALLOT AND CHESTNUT CRUNCH ROAST

This roast has everything you want in a hero dish: mouthwatering flavors and a great variety of textures. It is heavenly drizzled in gravy—the more the merrier! To prepare this roast ahead of time, store the filling in the fridge for up to three days, then proceed with the recipe as written.

Serves 6 to 8

For the Roast

1 package vegan filo pastry (I use Jus-Rol 10 x 18 inches [25 x 45 cm]; use a gluten-free kind if necessary)

1 tbsp (15 ml) olive oil

1¼ cups (200 g) finely sliced shallots

¾ cup (85 g) finely diced celery

¾ cup (83 g) finely grated carrot

3 tsp (15 g) minced garlic

1½ cups (210 g) precooked chestnuts

½ tsp sea salt

¼ tsp ground black pepper

2 tbsp (4 g) finely chopped fresh rosemary

2 tbsp (20 g) ground flaxseeds

1 tbsp (15 ml) apple cider vinegar

1 cup (175 g) mashed canned cannellini or butter beans

1 cup (90 g) rolled oats

For Serving

Brandy Peppercorn Sauce (page 140)

The Perfect Roast Potatoes (page 104)

Pecan and Apple Stuffing (page 107)

Take the filo pastry out of the refrigerator, so the layers can gently soften and become easier to handle while you prepare the rest of the roast.

Heat the olive oil in a large nonstick pan over medium heat and add the shallots. Cook them for 5 to 6 minutes, stirring regularly, until they have softened and begin to caramelize. Add the celery, carrot and garlic to the pan and cook over medium heat for 10 minutes to lightly caramelize the vegetables. Stir occasionally to prevent the mixture from burning. Carefully transfer it to a large mixing bowl.

In the meantime, preheat your oven to 375°F (190°C). Grease a 7-inch (18-cm) round cake pan. Finely slice half of the chestnuts and roughly chop the remaining half. This will give us a wonderful texture in this roast, but adjust to your preference!

Add the chestnuts, salt, pepper and rosemary to the mixing bowl. Sprinkle in the flaxseeds, then add the apple cider vinegar and white bean mash. Stir to combine, then fold in the oats. The mixture should be firm and sticky, not crumbly. If it's too dry, add a sprinkle of water. If it's too wet, add more oats until you get the desired texture.

Transfer the mixture to the prepared cake pan and firmly press the mixture into the pan, evening out the top.

Take individual sheets of filo pastry and gently crinkle them in your hand, then carefully press them onto the top of the nut roast. Repeat until all the filo sheets are placed on top. They should be packed firmly and touching one another.

Cover the pan with foil and roast for 30 minutes. Remove the foil and bake for 5 to 10 minutes, or until the filo pastry is golden.

Carefully remove the roast from the oven. Slide a long knife around the edges to gently remove it from the cake pan. Slice it like a cake and serve the individual pieces with a generous drizzle of your favorite gravy. I love this roast with brandy peppercorn sauce, and it's wonderful served alongside roast potatoes and stuffing.

CURRIED NUT ROAST

Nut roasts are a classic when it comes to vegan roast dinners, so of course I had to include a recipe for you in this book! I have included warming spices, such as turmeric, cumin and garam masala, to add a vibrant variety of notes to the otherwise simple roast. Roasts like these are perfect to make in advance and can easily be portioned and stored in the freezer.

Serves 4 to 6

For the Roast

2 tbsp (30 ml) olive oil

1 cup (160 g) finely diced yellow onion

½ tsp sea salt

2 tsp (10 g) crushed garlic

1 cup (150 g) shredded carrots

2½ cups (280 g) roughly chopped mixed nuts

1 (0.4-oz [11-g]) cube vegetable bouillon

1–2 tbsp (6–12 g) almond flour, to coat the loaf pan

¼ cup (64 g) peanut butter

2 tbsp (30 ml) fresh lemon juice

3 tbsp (45 ml) water

1 tbsp (6 g) curry powder

½ tsp ground cumin

½ tsp garam masala

½ tsp turmeric powder

¼ tsp ground black pepper

For Serving

Vegan Yorkies (page 108)

Miso Onion Gravy (page 139)

Heat the olive oil in a large, nonstick skillet over medium-high heat. Add the onion and cook for 2 minutes, until translucent. Add the salt and garlic. Cook for 2 minutes, then add the carrots. Stir to combine and cook for 3 to 4 minutes, or until the carrots begin to soften. Remove the pan from the heat.

Transfer the mixed nuts to a food processor and process for 10 to 20 seconds to roughly chop. Move the mixed nuts to a bowl and set it aside. Place a bouillon cube into your food processor and pulse until it's mostly broken up.

Preheat your oven to 375°F (190°C). Grease a 14 x 6–inch (35 x 15–cm) loaf pan and coat it with the almond flour.

To the food processor, add the peanut butter, lemon juice and water. Process until smooth. Sprinkle in the curry powder, cumin, garam masala, turmeric powder and black pepper. Blend for 1 minute to combine.

Add the carrot mixture, nuts and peanut butter blend to a large bowl and mix to combine. Transfer the nut roast into the loaf pan, gently pressing down to firmly pack it and even out the top.

Transfer the loaf to the preheated oven and bake for 25 to 30 minutes, or until it's golden on top. Remove it from the oven and allow the roast to cool for 10 minutes before carefully removing it from the loaf pan. Slice and serve alongside Yorkies and miso onion gravy.

STUFFED HASSELBACK SQUASH

We are taking squash to the next level with this gorgeous stuffed Hasselback squash! The idea of a Hasselback originated in Sweden in the 1950s. It is a technique of cutting a potato about halfway through into thin, fan-like slices and then baking it. In this recipe, I'm using this beautiful technique on butternut squash. It results in a stunning centerpiece for the roast dinner table—and it's a delicious one, filled with a creamy white wine stuffing. This recipe is also a great way to use up any leftover stale bread, and it can easily be made gluten-free by using gluten-free bread and breadcrumbs.

Serves 4 to 6

For the Squash

1 tbsp (15 ml) olive oil

½ cup (80 g) finely sliced shallots

½ tsp sea salt

1–2 tsp (5–10 g) crushed garlic

¼ cup (60 ml) vegan white wine

¾ cup (185 ml) dairy-free cream

2 tsp (3 g) dried sage

1 tbsp (5 g) nutritional yeast

¼ tsp ground black pepper

3.5 oz (100 g) cubed bread (roughly ¾-inch [2-cm] cubes)

1 butternut squash (35 oz [1 kg])

2 tbsp (14 g) breadcrumbs

Heat the olive oil in a large nonstick skillet over medium heat, then add the shallots. Sauté for 2 to 3 minutes, until softened. Sprinkle in the salt and add the garlic to the skillet. Cook for 2 minutes, stirring frequently. Deglaze the pan with the white wine and cook the mixture for 4 to 5 minutes, until the majority of the liquid reduces.

Pour in the dairy-free cream and combine well. Stir in the sage, nutritional yeast and black pepper. Reduce the heat to low and allow the mixture to simmer for 5 minutes.

Add the bread cubes to the skillet. Remove it from the heat and stir to coat the bread well in the sauce. Set the mixture aside while you prepare your squash.

Peel your butternut squash and cut it in half lengthwise. Spoon out all the seeds to create a pocket for the filling (refer to the photos on page 24). The size of the pocket can vary depending on the size of the butternut squash; I usually dig out a little more than just the seeds to create enough space for my filling. The scooped-out flesh is great to keep in a freezer bag for your next homemade broth—just saying!

Preheat your oven to 390°F (200°C) and line a baking sheet with parchment paper. Carefully spoon the creamy bread mixture into each half of the butternut squash until level. Give it a squeeze and ensure it's all tightly packed into the squash, then place the squash stuffed side down onto your baking sheet.

(continued)

For the Glaze

1 tbsp (15 ml) plant milk

1 tbsp (15 ml) tamari

For Serving

Miso Onion Gravy (page 139)

The Perfect Roast Potatoes (page 104) or Ranch Potato Mash (page 115)

Smoky Crusted Green Beans (page 131)

Use a sharp knife to carefully cut the Hasselback design into your squash, making sure not to cut all the way to the bottom so your squash halves are still connected in one piece. I like to place chopsticks to the left and right of the squash and then carefully cut thin slices until my knife hits the chopsticks. This prevents the knife from going all the way to the bottom and creates nice and even cuts. Definitely give this technique a go! You can also use other alternatives; just make sure they give you about ⅕ inch (5 mm) above your baking sheet, so you don't cut too deep.

Combine the plant milk and tamari for your glaze and brush it across your Hasselback squash. Sprinkle with the breadcrumbs, then transfer the squash to the hot oven and roast for 35 to 45 minutes, or until your squash is nicely golden with a slightly crispy top. To be sure it's cooked all the way through, poke it with a toothpick. The inside of your squash should be soft. If it's golden and crispy, but not cooked all the way through yet, reduce the heat to 320°F (160°C), cover with aluminum foil and cook for 10 to 15 minutes until tender.

Serve alongside your favorite gravy. I love the miso onion gravy with this Hasselback squash! It is best served with roast potatoes or ranch potato mash and green beans. Simply divine!

ROASTED EGGPLANT STEAK

You've probably never eaten eggplant in this way, but once you've tried it, you won't want to eat it any other way! We first char the eggplant skin to remove it. Then we rub the steaks in a flavorful rub and press them in a hot pan to release the moisture and condense the eggplant, creating a wonderfully meaty texture that easily takes on flavors. This is perfect for a roast-y date night as it serves two. It's also easy to scale up if you're looking to serve a bigger crowd!

Serves 2

For the Eggplant

2 eggplants (roughly 10.6 oz [300 g] each)

5 tbsp (75 ml) olive oil, divided

1 cup (240 ml) vegan red wine

1 tbsp (15 ml) tamari

For the Rub

1 tsp whole fennel seeds

1 tbsp (14 g) light brown sugar, packed

½ tsp smoked paprika

½ tsp onion powder

½ tsp smoked salt

½ tsp dried oregano

¼ tsp garlic powder

¼ tsp cayenne pepper

Wash your eggplants and cut off the stems, then char both whole eggplants over an open flame. I like to place them onto our gas stove and char them, carefully turning with barbecue tongs, until they are evenly blackened and softened all the way around. The skin should begin to peel off in places. It should take about 5 to 10 minutes for each eggplant.

Transfer the charred eggplants to an airtight container while still hot. Let them sit with the lid closed for at least 10 minutes. The eggplants will "sweat" and soften further. Remove the lid and peel off the skins.

If you don't have a gas stove, you can roast the eggplants in the oven under the broiler. Heat your oven on the broiler setting to about 390°F (200°C) for 5 minutes. Place the eggplants on an ovenproof dish on the top rack of your oven for 10 to 20 minutes, flipping them regularly to evenly char the eggplant skin all around. When done, carefully peel off the skin—but be careful: It's hot!

Preheat your oven to 390°F (200°C).

Place the fennel seeds in a hot, dry pan and toast them over medium heat for 3 to 4 minutes, or until fragrant. Transfer them to a spice grinder and process until finely ground—or crush them with a pestle and mortar. Mix the ground fennel seeds with the brown sugar, paprika, onion powder, smoked salt, oregano, garlic powder and cayenne pepper. Rub the mixture onto your eggplants and place them back in an ovenproof dish.

If you're preparing this dish ahead of time, you can place your rubbed eggplants in an airtight container and store them in the fridge overnight.

Drizzle the eggplants with 2 tablespoons (30 ml) of olive oil. Pour the red wine into the dish and roast the eggplants in the oven for 20 minutes.

(continued)

ROASTED EGGPLANT STEAK (CONTINUED)

For Serving

The Perfect Roast Potatoes (page 104)

Vegan Yorkies (page 108)

Roasted Sprouts with Smoky Tofu Bits (page 123)

Brandy Peppercorn Sauce (page 140)

When the eggplant is done roasting, remove it from the oven. Heat the remaining oil in a medium cast-iron pan over medium heat and add the eggplants. Place a second cast-iron pan on top and gently press down onto your eggplants for 3 to 4 minutes, until they start to sizzle and release their water. Once you get your eggplants to about ½ inch (1 cm) thick, remove the top pan and drizzle any leftover liquid from your baking dish over the eggplants.

Cook for 10 to 15 minutes, until the liquid reduces, carefully flipping the eggplants every 2 to 3 minutes. Brush the eggplants with the tamari on both sides, then remove from the heat. Serve the eggplant steaks immediately alongside roast potatoes, Yorkies, roasted sprouts and a delicious drizzle of brandy peppercorn sauce.

MINI APPLE AND SAGE ROASTIES

Apple and sage are a team made in heaven! Your kitchen will be filled with mouthwatering scents, calling everyone to the table in an instant. If you're gluten-free, make sure to use gluten-free oats in this recipe.

Serves 6

For the Roasties

3 whole (1-oz [28-g]) garlic bulbs

½ tbsp (7 ml) olive oil

2 tbsp (28 g) vegan butter, divided

¾ cup (120 g) finely diced yellow onion

½ tsp sea salt, plus more to taste

¼ cup (2 g) fresh sage leaves

2 cups (240 g) chopped apples

1 tbsp (15 ml) fresh lemon juice

2 tbsp (28 g) light brown sugar, packed

⅔ cup (78 g) pecans

1 tbsp (10 g) sunflower seeds

⅔ cup (70 g) rolled oats

Ground black pepper, to taste

For Serving

Miso Onion Gravy (page 139)

Smoky Crusted Green Beans (page 131)

Maple-Roasted Sweet Potatoes (page 111)

Preheat your oven to 375°F (190°C).

Cut the top ¼ inch (6 mm) off of each garlic bulb. Place the bulbs on a sheet of aluminum foil big enough to cover them. Drizzle the olive oil over the top and close the foil around the bulbs. Transfer them to the oven and roast for 25 to 30 minutes, or until fragrant and soft inside the foil. Remove the garlic and keep the oven preheated.

Add 1 tablespoon (14 g) of the vegan butter to a large, nonstick skillet and melt it over medium heat. Add the onion and the salt. Sauté for 4 to 5 minutes, until the onion is soft and translucent, then remove it from the skillet.

Add 1 tablespoon (14 g) of vegan butter to the skillet and heat it for 1 minute before adding the fresh sage leaves. Fry them for 1 to 2 minutes, or until they are fragrant. Add the apples, lemon juice, brown sugar and the cooked onion. Stir to combine.

Reduce the heat to low, then remove the roasted garlic from the foil. Carefully squeeze the garlic into a small bowl and mash with the back of a fork. Stir the garlic into the skillet and allow the mixture to cook for 5 to 7 minutes. Stir frequently while preparing the rest of the ingredients.

To a food processor, add the pecans, sunflower seeds and oats. Pulse 10 to 20 times to achieve your desired texture. Keep it chunky if you prefer! Pour the mixture into the skillet and remove it from the heat. Stir to combine. Season to taste with salt and pepper.

Add muffin liners to a six-hole muffin pan. Divide the mixture evenly among the liners and use the back of a spoon to firmly press the mixture down, then transfer the muffin pan to the preheated oven.

Bake for 20 to 25 minutes, or until golden on top. Allow the roasties to cool for 5 to 10 minutes before carefully removing them from the muffin pan and liners.

Serve with gravy alongside green beans and sweet potatoes.

ORANGE AND CRANBERRY ROAST WREATH

With the addition of orange, this roast is extra zesty and brings the deliciously sweet taste of cranberries to the next level. The stunning wreath shape will look beautiful on your festive dinner table!

Serves 6 to 8

For the Roast Wreath

2 tbsp (28 g) vegan butter

1 cup (160 g) finely diced red onion

2 tsp (10 g) crushed garlic

1 cup (101 g) finely diced celery

1 cup (128 g) finely diced carrots

1⅓ cups (130 g) cranberries

1 tsp orange zest

¼ cup (60 ml) fresh orange juice (roughly ½ medium orange)

½ tsp sea salt

1 tbsp (14 g) light brown sugar

1 tsp fresh thyme

1 (0.4-oz [11-g]) cube vegetable bouillon

¼ tsp ground black pepper

2 cups (234 g) chopped walnuts

2 tbsp (32 g) peanut butter

1 tbsp (15 ml) apple cider vinegar

2 tbsp (30 ml) water

2 tbsp (12 g) almond flour

2 tbsp (20 g) flaxseeds

4 tbsp (60 g) cranberry sauce

Orange shavings and nuts, to decorate the wreath (optional)

For Serving

Smoky Crusted Green Beans (page 131)

Brandy Peppercorn Sauce (page 140)

Place the vegan butter in a large, nonstick skillet over medium heat. Add the onion and sauté for 3 to 4 minutes, until softened. Add the garlic. Cook for 1 minute, then add the celery and carrots. Stir and cook for 8 to 10 minutes, or until the carrots have slightly softened.

Add the cranberries to the pan and stir to incorporate them. Cook the mixture for 5 minutes, or until the cranberries have softened. Reduce the heat to low. Stir in the orange zest, fresh orange juice, salt and brown sugar. After 2 minutes, add the fresh thyme. Crumble in the bouillon cube and add the black pepper. Simmer over low heat while you're preparing the rest of the ingredients.

In the meantime, transfer the walnuts to a food processor and pulse for 10 to 20 seconds to break them into chunks. Transfer them to the skillet, stir them in and remove the skillet from the heat.

Preheat your oven to 375°F (190°C). In a small bowl, whisk the peanut butter, apple cider vinegar and water. Add it to the skillet and stir all the ingredients together, then stir in the almond flour and flaxseeds.

Grease a 10½-inch (27-cm) ring cake pan and transfer the mixture to the cake pan. Firmly press it down into the ring with the back of a spoon or spatula to pack it densely. Carefully even out the top of the cake ring and transfer it to the preheated oven.

Bake for 30 to 35 minutes, turning the ring around halfway through to ensure it bakes evenly. Once the edges begin to brown, remove the cake ring from the oven.

Allow your wreath to cool on an even surface for 10 to 15 minutes before carefully turning it upside down on a serving dish and removing the cake ring.

Decorate the top of the wreath with cranberry sauce, along with orange shavings and nuts (if using). Serve this delicious and festive roast alongside green beans and brandy peppercorn sauce.

STICKY MUSHROOM STEAK

Packed full of natural umami flavor, mushrooms are definitely a hero on the dinner table! These sticky mushroom steaks use oyster cluster mushrooms as a base and the fabulous mushroom pressing technique created by my talented friend chef Derek Sarno of Wicked Healthy. In this technique, the mushroom clusters are pressed between two heavy cast-iron skillets while they are cooking, releasing their moisture and creating a succulent, meaty texture.

Serves 4

For the Steak

2 tbsp (28 g) vegan butter

4 oyster cluster mushrooms or the biggest chunks you can find (5.3 oz [150 g] each)

Pinch of sea salt

¼ tsp ground black pepper

1 tbsp (15 ml) tamari

½ cup (125 ml) vegan lager (gluten-free if needed)

For the Sauce

1 tsp liquid smoke

1 cup (240 ml) tomato passata

½ tsp garlic powder

1 tsp onion powder

1 tsp porcini mushroom powder (optional)

1 tbsp (15 ml) fresh lemon juice

1 tsp cayenne pepper or chili powder

1 tbsp (15 ml) maple syrup

For Serving

Parsnip and Miso Mash (page 124)

Brandy Peppercorn Sauce (page 140)

Line a baking sheet with parchment paper or a nonstick baking mat.

Melt the vegan butter in a large cast-iron skillet over medium heat. Add the mushrooms, sprinkle them with salt and black pepper and fry for 2 minutes. Then place a second cast-iron skillet of the same size on top of the first and cook the mushrooms for 20 minutes with the top pan pressed down on them.

After 20 minutes, gently press down the top skillet with a kitchen towel. During this cooking time, the mushrooms will release their liquid and lightly caramelize. This will press them into nice, firm and condensed mushroom steaks.

After 5 minutes of pressing, carefully flip the mushroom steaks and press on the second side for roughly 5 minutes, or until the mushrooms are lightly charred. Remove the second skillet and keep it on the heat for 5 minutes, or until the majority of the liquid evaporates from the skillet.

Increase the heat to high, then pour the tamari over the steaks. Flip the mushrooms after about 30 seconds and pour in the vegan lager. This will deglaze the skillet. Cook for 3 to 4 minutes, until most of the liquid has evaporated. Remove from the heat instantly, then transfer the mushroom steaks to the baking sheet.

Preheat your oven to 375°F (190°C).

In the meantime, prepare your sauce: In a medium-sized bowl, combine the liquid smoke, tomato passata, garlic powder, onion powder, porcini mushroom powder (if using), lemon juice, cayenne pepper and maple syrup. Stir in any leftover liquid from the skillet into the sauce.

Brush the mushroom steaks thickly with the sauce on both sides, then bake them for 12 to 15 minutes. Serve immediately. These sticky mushroom steaks are simply divine alongside parsnip mash and drizzled with brandy peppercorn sauce.

MINI RAINBOW WELLINGTONS

What I love most about these Mini Rainbow Wellingtons is their vibrant color, but the fact that they are pre-portioned and look stunning on a dinner plate is pretty wonderful too! Use gluten-free puff pastry for this recipe, if needed. These are also perfect for making ahead of time: Assemble them and place them in your freezer instead of the oven. They are a quick bake on the day you wish to serve them.

Serves 3

For the Wellingtons

2 sheets vegan puff pastry
(I use Jus-Rol 14 x 9 inches
[35 x 23 cm])

7 oz (200 g) thinly sliced fresh beetroot (1–2 mm thick)

7 oz (200 g) peeled and thinly sliced sweet potato (1–2 mm thick)

7 oz (200 g) peeled and thinly sliced carrot (1–2 mm thick)

7 oz (200 g) peeled and thinly sliced white potato (1–2 mm thick)

4 oz (113 g) thinly sliced large broccoli stem (1–2 mm thick)

1 tbsp (15 ml) tamari

2 tbsp (30 ml) plant milk

2–3 tbsp (18–27 g) sesame seeds (optional)

For Serving

Shredded BBQ Cabbage
(page 127)

Smoky Crusted Green Beans
(page 131)

Brandy Peppercorn Sauce
(page 140)

Remove the puff pastry from the fridge and let it rest at room temperature for at least 30 minutes to soften.

Gently unroll your sheets on a nonstick surface; parchment paper or a silicone baking mat works well. Use a 5-inch (13-cm) bowl upside down to cut even circles out of your puff pastry sheets. You will have six in total. Keep any leftover pastry for decorating the Wellingtons.

Steam the veggies for 4 to 5 minutes in a steamer on the stove. Carefully remove the slices and layer them onto three of the puff pastry rounds, leaving about ½ inch (1 cm) free around the edge. Layer them to about 2 to 3 inches (5 to 8 cm) thick, giving each vegetable an equal layer. I like to start with the vibrant beetroot at the bottom, then add sweet potato, carrot, white potato and finish off with the green broccoli stem.

Preheat your oven to 375°F (190°C).

Combine the tamari and plant milk in a small bowl. Brush it around the edges of each loaded pastry circle. Gently place a second pastry circle on top, allowing it to slightly stretch to reach the bottom edges. Gently press down the edges with your fingers, roll up the pastry edges and seal with the back of a fork.

To decorate your mini Wellingtons: Use cookie cutters or a sharp knife to create fun shapes. Brush the pastry with a little of the tamari and plant milk, then gently press it onto the mini Wellington to attach it.

Before transferring them to the oven, brush your pastry with the remaining tamari and plant milk mixture, and sprinkle with sesame seeds (if using) for an extra crunch.

Bake for 20 to 25 minutes, or until the pastry is golden. Allow to cool for 5 minutes before removing the Wellingtons from your baking sheet. Serve these alongside BBQ cabbage and green beans and drizzle with brandy peppercorn sauce.

STUFFED CABBAGE ROLLS

This is one of those classic German dishes I remember from Sunday lunches with the family. To this day, my mum cooks them regularly on the weekend. Like my mum's traditional recipe, these are created with savoy cabbage leaves, gently steamed and softened, then stuffed with mushrooms, walnuts and black beans before roasting for an earthy umami flavor.

Serves 6

For the Cabbage Rolls

2½ cups (400 g) chestnut mushrooms

1 tsp sea salt

1¾ cups (200 g) walnuts

⅓ cup (55 g) black beans

⅓ cup (22 g) finely chopped fresh parsley

½ tsp smoked paprika

¼ tsp ground black pepper

1 tsp onion powder

6–8 savoy cabbage leaves

1 cup (240 ml) vegetable stock

4–5 sprigs fresh herbs, such as sage, rosemary and thyme

2 tbsp (30 ml) olive oil, for frying

For Serving

The Perfect Roast Potatoes (page 104)

Creamy Cauliflower Bake with Caramelized Onions (page 112)

Red Wine Gravy (page 136)

Place the chestnut mushrooms in a food processor and pulse for roughly 15 seconds to break them down. Transfer them to a dry skillet over medium-high heat, sprinkle with the salt and cook the mushrooms for 15 to 20 minutes, stirring frequently. After a few minutes, they will begin to release their water. Continue to cook them until the majority of the liquid has evaporated.

In the meantime, transfer the walnuts to the food processor and pulse for 15 seconds. In a small bowl, mash the black beans with the back of a fork. Add the beans and walnuts to the skillet and remove it from the heat. Add the parsley, smoked paprika, black pepper and onion powder to the mixture. Stir to combine.

In a large saucepan, bring 35 ounces (1 L) of water to a boil. Place a steaming basket or a colander on top. Steam your savoy cabbage leaves for 5 minutes each, until softened. Carefully remove them from the saucepan and lay them flat on an even surface.

Preheat your oven to 375°F (190°C).

Divide the mushroom mixture between all the cabbage leaves, spooning it into the middle of each leaf. Place the leaf in your palm and fold the left and right edges over the filling, gently pressing to keep it together. Then roll up the top and bottom of each leaf and secure with a food-safe string.

Transfer all the cabbage rolls to an ovenproof dish. Pour over the vegetable stock and place the fresh herbs in the dish.

Roast at 375°F (190°C) for 15 minutes, then remove from the oven.

Heat the olive oil in a large, nonstick pan over medium-high heat, gently remove each cabbage roll from the ovenproof dish and fry it in the pan for 3 to 4 minutes on each side, until golden on both sides. Repeat until all the cabbage rolls are done. Serve immediately alongside roast potatoes, creamy cauliflower bake and red wine gravy.

WILD MUSHROOM LOAF

There can never be enough mushrooms on the dinner table, if you ask me. I like to sneak them into my dishes as much as possible, as they add delicious depth to each meal. This loaf reminds me of a typical nut roast, being baked in a loaf shape—and it's not far off as we are adding almond, cashew and flaxseeds. The freshly cooked wild mushrooms take this to a whole other level and add the perfect texture and deliciously earthy notes to this mouthwatering hero of a dish.

Serves 6 to 8

For the Mushroom Loaf

3⅓ cups (500 g) mixed wild mushrooms of your choice (I used a blend of oyster, maitake, king oyster and shiitake)

½ tsp sea salt

¼ cup (60 ml) vegan white wine

¼ tsp ground black pepper

2 tbsp (8 g) fresh parsley, plus more for optional garnish

1 tbsp (14 g) vegan butter

½ cup (80 g) finely diced shallots

1⅔ cups (212 g) finely diced carrots

1 cup (101 g) finely diced celery

2 tsp (10 g) crushed garlic

1¼ cups (120 g) almond flour

2 tbsp (20 g) flaxseeds

1 cup (129 g) roughly chopped cashews

7 oz (198 ml) vegetable stock

5 cups (150 g) fresh spinach

For Serving

The Perfect Roast Potatoes (page 104)

Crunchy Rutabaga Fingers (page 128)

Your favorite gravy

Place the wild mushrooms in a large, dry skillet. Cook them over high heat, stirring frequently, for 10 to 12 minutes. After 5 minutes, sprinkle in the salt.

Deglaze the pan with the white wine, then stir in the black pepper and fresh parsley. Cook for 3 to 4 minutes, or until the majority of the liquid has evaporated. Remove the mushrooms from the skillet and set them aside.

Place the vegan butter in the skillet, then add the shallots, carrots and celery. Cook for 10 minutes, or until the carrots have softened, then stir through the garlic.

Sprinkle in the almond flour, flaxseeds and cashews. Pour in the vegetable stock and allow the mixture to simmer over low heat for 15 minutes. Add the spinach in batches and cook until wilted, then remove the mixture from the stove.

Preheat your oven to 375°F (190°C). Line and grease a 14 x 6-inch (35 x 15–cm) loaf pan.

Transfer the mixture to the pan. Even it out with a spatula, pressing down firmly to neatly pack the loaf pan. Bake for 25 to 30 minutes, or until the top is nicely golden. Allow the roast to cool for 10 minutes, before carefully turning it upside down on a serving platter. Top with the parsley, if using, before slicing.

Serve each slice with a side of roast potatoes, rutabaga fingers and your favorite gravy!

BBQ-ROASTED PINEAPPLE

Pineapple on a roast dinner? Heck yes! Hear me out: The juicy, caramelized sweetness of this BBQ pineapple is divine. And it pairs wonderfully with shredded BBQ cabbage and maple-roasted sweet potatoes, keeping the sweet-savory theme going for the perfect meal! So, if this is up your street, you'll want to give roasted pineapple a go!

Serves 6

For the Pineapple

1 whole pineapple (roughly 1⅔ lb [800 g])

3 tbsp (45 ml) vegetable oil

4 tsp (20 g) sliced garlic

½ cup (125 ml) dark rum

For the BBQ Sauce

½ cup (144 ml) ketchup

1 tbsp (15 g) dark brown sugar, packed

1 tbsp (15 ml) apple cider vinegar

2 tsp (10 ml) molasses

1 tbsp (15 ml) tamari

¼ tsp chili flakes

1 tsp vegan Worcestershire sauce

For Serving

Maple-Roasted Sweet Potatoes (page 111)

Shredded BBQ Cabbage (page 127)

Remove the peel of your pineapple, then cut the pineapple into 1-inch (2.5-cm) slices. Use a round cookie cutter to remove the pineapple core from your slices.

Heat the vegetable oil in a large, nonstick skillet over medium heat. Add the garlic and cook for 2 minutes, or until fragrant. Remove the garlic from the skillet, leaving as much oil as possible. Add the pineapple steaks and fry for 12 to 15 minutes, flipping frequently, until golden and lightly caramelized on both sides. Remove from the heat.

Whip up your BBQ sauce: Combine the ketchup, brown sugar, apple cider vinegar, molasses, tamari, chili flakes and Worcestershire sauce.

Place the fried pineapple slices in a shallow dish and pour the rum over the top. Marinate for at least 1 hour or overnight.

Preheat your oven to 375°F (190°C). Grease a large, ovenproof dish.

Remove the pineapple slices from the rum and place them in the dish in a single layer. Spread three-quarters of the sauce across your pineapple slices. Roast them in the oven for 12 to 15 minutes, or until the sauce has lightly browned. Carefully flip your pineapple slices and spread the remaining sauce on the other side.

Roast for 12 to 15 minutes, until golden. Serve alongside maple-roasted sweet potato and BBQ cabbage.

ROASTED CABBAGE STEAKS

These cabbage steaks are a super quick and easy addition to the feasting table. I love to make them when there's little time to prepare a delicious feast—or when the guests are about to arrive and I realize something is missing. Cabbage turns deliciously sweet and succulent when it's roasted. In this recipe, I'm topping my cabbage with a smoky tomato crust and shredded vegan cheese. The cheese becomes melty and gooey in the oven and works wonders alongside the soft and chewy layers of the juicy cabbage.

Serves 4

For the Steaks

56 oz (1.6 kg) white cabbage

3 tbsp (48 g) tomato paste

2 tbsp (30 ml) vegan red wine

2 tbsp (30 ml) tamari

1 tbsp (15 ml) olive oil

¼ tsp garlic powder

½ tsp smoked paprika

1 cup (113 g) shredded vegan cheese

For Serving

Garlic Butter Mushroom Scallops (page 119)

Crunchy Rutabaga Fingers (page 128)

Roasted Red Pepper Gravy (page 144)

Preheat your oven to 375°F (190°C). Line a baking sheet with parchment paper.

Wash your cabbage and remove the outer two leaves, then slice your cabbage into 1-inch (2.5-cm) slices. Arrange your cabbage discs flatly on the lined baking tray in a single layer.

In a small bowl, combine the tomato paste, red wine, tamari, olive oil, garlic powder and smoked paprika. Spread it across your cabbage slices with the back of a spoon.

Transfer the baking sheet to the preheated oven and roast the cabbage steaks for 20 minutes. Carefully remove the tray from the oven and sprinkle your cabbage steaks with vegan shredded cheese. Return them to the oven for 12 to 15 minutes, or until the edges of the cabbage are browning and the vegan cheese has melted.

Serve these cabbage steaks alongside mushroom scallops, rutabaga fingers and roasted red pepper gravy.

TOFU AND CO. HEROES

This chapter is filled with appetizing and succulent tofu, tempeh or jackfruit dishes. Bland? No way. Full of flavor? Heck yes! Since going vegan and finding my creativity in the kitchen, I've been asked numerous times about how to make tofu and its companions taste great. It seems—despite tofu being around for over 2,000 years—there are still some everyday struggles with preparing this amazing ingredient to suit everyone's taste buds. Personally, I've loved tofu since day one when I first tried it as a kid, and I have been using it in all kinds of recipes throughout the years.

In this chapter, you will find some easy-to-follow, step-by-step guidance on how to turn tofu, jackfruit or tempeh into a delicious roast-worthy feast. If you're looking for a place to start, try the Orange and Ginger Glazed Tofu (page 46) or the Jackfruit Pot Roast (page 50). They are two of my favorites from this part of the book.

ORANGE AND GINGER GLAZED TOFU

Tofu is *never* boring in our household. For this festive dish, I've combined the flavors of zesty orange and zingy ginger in a delicious marinade and sticky glaze to make the tofu the hero of the plate. I love cooking with tofu because it's so versatile and allows for getting creative in the kitchen. With a few simple steps, you can easily make tofu taste fantastic!

Serves 2 to 3

For the Tofu

1 (14-oz [400-g]) block extra-firm tofu, drained

Olive oil, for frying

3 tbsp (24 g) cornstarch

Orange and Ginger Marinade

2 tbsp (30 ml) olive oil

3 cloves garlic, sliced

½ cup (125 ml) fresh orange juice (roughly 1 medium orange)

¼ cup (60 ml) maple syrup

¼ cup (60 ml) tamari

1 tsp liquid smoke

1 (1-inch [2.5-cm]) piece fresh ginger, finely grated

½ tsp ground black pepper

For Serving

Smoky Crusted Green Beans (page 131)

Parsnip and Miso Mash (page 124)

Miso Onion Gravy (page 139)

Press your tofu block for at least 30 minutes. This step is optional, but the tofu takes on the flavors of the marinade better when it's pressed.

In the meantime, prepare your marinade: In a small saucepan, heat your olive oil over low heat. Add the garlic slices. Heat them for 5 minutes, stirring frequently to ensure the garlic does not turn brown. Remove the pan from the heat and set it aside.

In a large bowl, add the orange juice, maple syrup, tamari, liquid smoke, ginger and black pepper. Strain the garlic oil through a sieve to remove the garlic pieces. Discard the garlic and add the garlic oil to the marinade. Stir to combine.

Use a sharp knife to cut diagonal lines across the top and bottom of your pressed tofu, about ¼ inch (6 mm) deep. Place the tofu in a small container and add your marinade so that it covers the tofu. Place it in the fridge to marinate for 30 minutes.

Preheat your oven to 390°F (200°C). Heat a large, nonstick skillet over medium heat with a generous dash of olive oil. Remove your tofu from the marinade and allow for any excess to drip off the tofu block.

Sprinkle the cornstarch onto a shallow plate and place the tofu block on top, thinly coating the top and bottom. Transfer the tofu block to the frying plan and fry both sides of the tofu for 2 to 3 minutes each, until crispy and golden. Place it into an ovenproof dish.

Whisk about 2 teaspoons (5 g) of the cornstarch into the remainder of the marinade and pour about half of the marinade over the tofu. Roast for 10 minutes, then carefully pour the rest of the marinade over the top and roast for 10 minutes.

Remove the tofu from the ovenproof dish and place it onto a serving plate. Cut it into ½-inch (1-cm) slices and serve as part of your roast meal. Try this with green beans, a parsnip mash and some delicious miso onion gravy.

STICKY FRIED TOFU STEAKS

This is next-level tofu: With a crispy fried skin and a sticky roasted tomato and red wine sauce, these succulent tofu steaks are simply divine! They're panfried and caramelized to give them the crunchy outer layer, then they're oven-roasted in the flavorful sauce to turn them into irresistible vegan comfort food.

Serves 4

For the Tofu

2 (14-oz [400-g]) blocks extra-firm tofu

2 tbsp (30 ml) olive oil

½ cup (125 ml) vegan red wine, divided

For the Sauce

½ cup (125 ml) tomato passata

½ cup (125 ml) vegan red wine, divided

2 tbsp (30 ml) tamari

½ cup (125 ml) vegetable stock

1 tbsp (15 ml) olive oil

1 tbsp (15 ml) liquid smoke

1 tsp onion powder

½ tsp garlic powder

½ tsp smoked paprika

¼ tsp ground black pepper

1 tbsp (3 g) dried sage

For Serving

Chilli Cheeze Corn Bread Dumplings (page 116)

Roasted Sprouts with Smoky Tofu Bits (page 123)

Maple-Roasted Sweet Potatoes (page 111)

Press both tofu blocks for 1 hour to remove any excess liquid.

In a medium-sized bowl, whisk the tomato passata, red wine, tamari, vegetable stock, olive oil, liquid smoke, onion powder, garlic powder, smoked paprika, black pepper and dried sage until well combined.

Preheat your oven to 375°F (190°C). Heat the olive oil in a medium cast-iron pan over medium-high heat. Fry both pressed tofu blocks for 4 to 5 minutes on each side, until they start creating a crispy crust. Remove them from the pan and carefully score the top in a crisscross pattern. Place them back into the hot pan, scored side facing down.

Pour ¼ cup (60 ml) of the red wine into the hot pan and allow it to simmer for 10 minutes over medium-low heat.

Press the tofu steaks gently into the pan with a ladle or spoon and cook for 12 to 15 minutes, until the red wine begins to caramelize and the liquid has mostly evaporated. Flip the steaks, add the remaining red wine to deglaze the pan and pour the mixed sauce over the tofu steaks.

Transfer the cast-iron pan into the oven at 375°F (190°C) and roast for 10 to 15 minutes, or until the sauce thickens and the edges of the tofu steaks become golden.

Carefully remove the hot pan from the oven, then serve up your tofu steaks sliced and drizzled with the thickened cooking sauce. These tofu steaks are perfect served alongside corn bread dumplings, roasted sprouts and sweet potatoes.

JACKFRUIT POT ROAST

Jackfruit is an amazing ingredient, and its versatility shines through when it comes to creating roast dinners! This jackfruit pot roast is so hearty and reminds me of Sunday roasts with the German family. Throughout the cooking process, the jackfruit becomes beautifully soft, juicy and tender. It takes on all the flavors of the sauce surrounding it, making it a wonderful ingredient for this pot roast!

Serves 4 to 6

For the Roast

1 tbsp (15 ml) olive oil

7 oz (198 g) roughly chopped yellow onion

¾ tsp sea salt, divided

3 tsp (15 g) crushed garlic

3 (7.4-oz [210-g]) cans jackfruit, drained

¼ cup (60 ml) brandy

1 cup (240 ml) vegan red wine

¼ tsp ground black pepper

1 tbsp (15 ml) balsamic vinegar

1 tbsp (3 g) dried rosemary

1 tsp dried thyme

1 tsp dried sage

1 tbsp (8 g) cornstarch

2 cups (473 ml) vegetable stock

30 oz (850 g) mixed peeled and roughly chopped vegetables (I like to use potato, carrot and parsnip)

Fresh parsley, to serve (optional)

For Serving

The Perfect Roast Potatoes (page 104)

Vegan Yorkies (page 108)

Parsnip and Miso Mash (page 124)

Heat the olive oil in a large, nonstick skillet over medium heat. Add the yellow onion and sprinkle in ½ teaspoon of salt. Sauté for 5 minutes, or until tender.

Add the garlic and cook for 1 minute, then add the drained jackfruit. Cook for 8 to 10 minutes over medium heat, stirring frequently, until the jackfruit begins to soften. Deglaze the pan with the brandy, then pour in the red wine.

Preheat your oven to 375°F (190°C). Sprinkle the black pepper and remaining salt into the pan. Add the balsamic vinegar, rosemary, thyme and sage. Stir to combine, then cook for 5 minutes.

In a bowl, stir the cornstarch into the vegetable stock, then pour the mixture into the pan with the jackfruit. Stir to combine. Place the vegetables in a casserole dish. Pour in the jackfruit and sauce mixture, and cover with a lid or aluminum foil.

Roast for 30 to 35 minutes. Give the pot roast a stir and sprinkle it with fresh parsley (if using) before serving it alongside roast potatoes, Yorkies and parsnip mash.

JACKFRUIT FILO MINI WELLINGTONS

With its outer crunchy filo pastry and soft, hearty filling, these mini Wellingtons are truly a festival of textures! The full-bodied filling is created with tender jackfruit and fresh spinach and seasoned with tangy, sweet balsamic vinegar. It's all coated in flaky filo pastry that becomes super crunchy in the oven.

Serves 4 (makes 4 parcels)

For the Wellingtons

2 tbsp (30 ml) olive oil

1 cup (189 g) finely diced yellow onion

½ tsp sea salt

4–5 tsp (20–25 g) crushed garlic

2 (7.2-oz [210-g]) cans shredded jackfruit, drained

5 cups (150 g) fresh spinach

1 tbsp (6 g) mushroom powder

½ tsp ground black pepper

¼ cup (60 ml) balsamic vinegar, plus 1 tbsp (15 ml) for the "egg" wash

1 package vegan filo pastry (I use Jus-Rol 10 x 18 inches [25 x 45 cm])

2 tbsp (30 ml) melted vegan butter

1–2 tbsp (9–18 g) sesame seeds (optional)

For Serving

Steamed or roasted vegetables

Parsnip and Miso Mash (page 124) or Savory Sweet Potato–Peanut Crumble (page 120)

Red Wine Gravy (page 136)

Heat the olive oil in a large, nonstick skillet over medium heat. Sauté the onion for 3 to 4 minutes, until it begins to soften. Sprinkle in the salt and add the garlic. Cook for 5 minutes, until translucent. Stir in the shredded jackfruit and cook for 5 minutes, stirring frequently.

Add the fresh spinach to the skillet and cook for 2 to 3 minutes while stirring, until the spinach is wilted and well combined and reduce the heat to low.

Sprinkle in the mushroom powder and black pepper, then drizzle in the balsamic vinegar. Mix to combine, then remove the skillet from the heat and allow the mixture to cool almost completely for at least 30 minutes.

Unroll the filo pastry sheets and gently separate the layers. Place one layer on a cutting board, brush it with the melted vegan butter and top with the next layer of filo pastry. Repeat until you have four layers on top of each other, then cut the sheets into a 5 x 12–inch (13 x 30–cm) rectangle.

Preheat your oven to 360°F (182°C). Line a baking sheet with parchment paper.

Transfer 3 tablespoons (about 30 g) of the cooled down jackfruit mixture onto the filo layers, placing them in the middle of the shorter edge and leaving about ½ inch (1 cm) free on each side. Carefully roll up the filo parcel, firmly pressing the edges together to seal, then place your parcels on the baking sheet.

Brush the parcels with 1 tablespoon (15 ml) of balsamic vinegar and sprinkle over some sesame seeds (if using). Then transfer the tray to the oven and roast your parcels for 20 to 25 minutes, until crispy around the edges.

Serve the jackfruit parcels alongside steamed or roasted vegetables and parsnip mash or savory potato crumble. Don't forget to drizzle with red wine gravy—delicious! Any leftover parcels are also tasty cold or reheated the next day.

STICKY TEMPEH PARCELS

Tempeh is a delicious ingredient in stir-fries and fantastic to use in roasts! Tofu is made from soy curdles, and tempeh is made from fermented soybeans. It brings its own aromas into the recipe, and it's also a great ingredient to soak up any marinade flavors. For these sticky tempeh parcels, we're marinating the tempeh in a sweet and smoky tomato sauce for at least 4 hours and ideally overnight, so the tempeh can take on as much of the aroma as possible. The tempeh is then wrapped in softened rice paper and roasted in the thickened sauce to resemble a crunchy outer skin that the sauce will stick to just perfectly! A 100 percent yum factor! To make these gluten-free, use gluten-free breadcrumbs in the recipe.

Serves 6 to 8

For the Tempeh Parcels

2 (7-oz [200-g]) blocks tempeh

½ cup (125 ml) soymilk or other plant milk

8 (8.6 x 8.6–inch [22 x 22–cm]) rice paper sheets

1 tbsp (15 ml) vegetable oil

1 tsp cornstarch

½ cup (125 ml) water

2 tbsp (14 g) breadcrumbs

For the Marinade

¼ cup (60 ml) vegetable oil

¼ cup (60 ml) tomato passata

2 tbsp (30 ml) tamari

1 tbsp (7 g) onion powder

1 tsp garlic powder

½ tsp smoked paprika

2 tbsp (30 ml) maple syrup

1 tsp vegan steak seasoning

For Serving

Smoky Crusted Green Beans (page 131)

The Perfect Roast Potatoes (page 104)

Cut your tempeh blocks into eight 2-inch (5-cm) squares that are roughly 1 inch (2.5 cm) thick.

In an airtight container, combine the ingredients for your marinade: oil, passata, tamari, onion powder, garlic powder, smoked paprika, maple syrup and steak seasoning. Place your tempeh squares in the marinade and ensure they are evenly coated. Place the closed container in the fridge and marinate overnight or for at least 4 hours.

When the tempeh is ready, pour the soymilk onto a shallow plate big enough for the rice paper. Soak each rice paper sheet one by one in the plant milk for 1 to 2 minutes, then carefully lift each sheet and allow for any excess to drip off. Remove a tempeh square from the marinade, but don't discard the marinade yet! Place the tempeh in the middle of the softened rice paper and gently wrap the rice paper around it.

Preheat your oven to 375°F (190°C). Grease a large ovenproof dish.

Heat the oil in a large, nonstick pan and place each tempeh parcel in the pan, frying it for 10 to 15 minutes, flipping halfway through until both sides are lightly crispy. Transfer the tempeh parcels to the ovenproof dish.

Whisk the cornstarch and water into the remaining marinade, then pour the mixture over the tempeh parcels. Sprinkle the breadcrumbs on top of the parcels and roast for 20 to 25 minutes, or until golden with lightly browning edges.

Serve alongside the remaining sauce, green beans and roast potatoes.

NUT-CRUSTED ZESTY TOFU

This zesty and nutty tofu is definitely one to try! The tofu is seasoned in a white wine marinade that is later turned into a deliciously creamy light sauce. This recipe is best prepared in advance: Press your tofu, then marinate it in the fridge overnight or up to 3 days. If you're in a rush, 2 hours is fine. On the day of serving, sear the tofu, add the crumb and roast it before serving.

Serves 4

For the Tofu
2 (14-oz [400-g]) blocks extra-firm tofu
¼ cup (60 ml) olive oil

For the Marinade
10.8 oz (300 ml) vegan white wine
2 tsp (10 g) white miso paste
2 tsp (10 ml) mirin
¼ tsp white pepper
1 tsp sea salt
¼ cup (60 ml) fresh lemon juice

For the Nut Crumb
1 cup (100 g) walnuts
2 tbsp (18 g) fine breadcrumbs
2 tbsp (10 g) nutritional yeast
2 (3 x 2–inch [7.5 x 5–cm]) pieces nori, crushed
2 tbsp (10 g) fresh parsley
½ tsp sea salt
2 tsp (10 ml) olive oil

For the Sauce
2 tbsp (30 g) all-purpose flour
½ cup (125 ml) water
⅔ cup (158 ml) soy cream

For Serving
Garlic Butter Mushroom Scallops (page 119)
Roasted Sprouts with Smoky Tofu Bits (page 123)

Press both tofu blocks for 30 minutes to remove any excess liquid. In the meantime, whisk up the marinade in a bowl by combining the white wine, white miso paste, mirin, white pepper, salt and lemon juice.

Place both pressed tofu blocks in an airtight container and cover in the marinade. If needed, add a little extra white wine until the tofu is fully submerged. Cover the container and marinate for at least 2 hours or overnight.

Heat the olive oil in a large, nonstick skillet over medium heat. Add the tofu blocks to the skillet and set the marinade aside for later use. Fry the tofu blocks in the skillet on each side for 5 to 10 minutes, or until lightly crispy.

To create the crumb, add the walnuts to a food processor and pulse for 1 minute until the walnuts are broken down. Add the breadcrumbs, nutritional yeast, nori, fresh parsley, sea salt and olive oil. Pulse for 20 to 30 seconds to combine everything into a fine crumb.

Preheat your oven to 350°F (178°C).

In the meantime, make the sauce: Mix the flour with the water, then whisk it into the existing marinade and heat on the stove, simmering for 10 minutes, stirring frequently, until the sauce begins to thicken. Stir in the soy cream and cook for 2 minutes, then remove from the heat.

Transfer the tofu blocks to an ovenproof dish and sprinkle the nutty crumb over the top. Roast for 20 minutes. Carefully remove the tofu from the ovenproof dish and slice both blocks into ½-inch (1-cm) pieces. Drizzle with the sauce to serve. These nut-crusted tofu slices are delicious served alongside mushroom scallops and roasted sprouts.

STUFFED TOFU ROAST WITH SPINACH AND WALNUTS

I bet you've never made a tofu roast in this way! For this recipe, the tofu is baked with a creamy, nutty spinach-and-walnut filling. This can be made in advance and stored in the freezer.

Serves 6 to 8

For the Tofu

2 (14-oz [400-g]) blocks extra-firm tofu

1 tbsp plus 1 tsp (20 g) tomato paste

1 tsp crushed garlic

1 tbsp (15 ml) olive oil

2 tsp (10 g) vegan poultry seasoning

1 tbsp (15 ml) tamari

2 tbsp (10 g) nutritional yeast

3 tbsp (45 ml) balsamic vinegar

For the Filling

1 tbsp (15 ml) olive oil

6 oz (170 g) chopped yellow onion

1 tsp finely chopped garlic

⅔ cup (56 g) finely chopped celery

¾ cup (85 g) chopped walnuts

½ cup (71 g) nutritional yeast

¼ tsp ground black pepper

6 oz (170 g) frozen spinach

4 oz (118 ml) vegetable stock

1 cup (60 g) chopped fresh parsley

1–2 tbsp (6–12 g) almond flour

For Serving

Vegan Yorkies (page 108)

Your favorite gravy!

Place the tofu in a food processor with the tomato paste, garlic, olive oil, poultry seasoning, tamari and nutritional yeast. Process for 1 to 2 minutes, or until the mixture is smooth. If needed, take little breaks to scrape down the sides of the food processor with a spatula. Then set the mixture aside.

To create the filling, heat the olive oil in a large, nonstick skillet over medium heat and add the onion. Sauté for 3 to 4 minutes until soft, then add the garlic and celery. Cook for 2 minutes, stirring frequently.

Sprinkle in the walnuts, nutritional yeast and black pepper. Stir to combine, then add the frozen spinach. Simmer over low heat for 8 to 12 minutes, until the spinach softens. Pour in the vegetable stock and cook for 3 to 4 minutes. Sprinkle in the fresh parsley, stir and remove from the heat after 1 minute.

To thicken the sauce, stir in the almond flour and adjust the amount depending on how watery your spinach and parsley were.

Preheat your oven to 390°F (200°C). Line a 14 x 6–inch (35 x 15–cm) greased loaf pan with parchment paper.

Spread about three-quarters of the tofu mixture on the bottom and the walls of the loaf pan to about ½ inch (1 cm) thick, then fill the middle with the spinach mixture. Close the roast with the rest of the tofu mixture, until the filling is completely encapsulated in the tofu mix. Cover the loaf pan with aluminum foil and bake for 20 minutes, then reduce the heat to 300°F (150°C) for 5 minutes and remove the cover.

Allow the loaf to cool for at least 2 hours before removing it from the loaf pan. If you're planning to freeze the loaf, now is the perfect moment!

To heat the loaf, turn it upside down onto an ovenproof dish and brush the outside of the loaf with the balsamic vinegar. Bake the loaf at 320°F (160°C) in a preheated oven for 15 minutes, until golden. Slice to serve alongside Yorkies and your favorite gravy!

ROASTED SESAME TEMPEH FINGERS

Over the past couple of years, tempeh has easily become one of my favorite ingredients to cook with. It has a great bite and takes on any flavor you marinate it in, making it easy to season and adjust to your personal taste. These roasted sesame tempeh fingers are coated in a crunchy layer of sesame seeds. They are great for both drizzling in gravy and also dipping into delicious dips, such as the accompanying peanut sauce—simply delicious!

Serves 4

For the Tempeh

2 (7-oz [200-g]) blocks tempeh

¾–1 cup (108–144 g) sesame seeds

For the Marinade

½ cup (125 ml) vegan red wine

2 tbsp (30 ml) tamari

¼ cup (60 ml) peanut oil

1 tbsp (16 g) smooth peanut butter

1 tbsp (5 g) chili flakes

For the Sauce

¼ cup (64 g) smooth peanut butter

2 tbsp (30 ml) tamari

1 tbsp (15 ml) apple cider vinegar

1 tsp tomato paste

½ tsp chili flakes

1 tsp cornstarch

½ cup (125 ml) water

For Serving

Parsnip and Miso Mash (page 124)

Savory Sweet Potato–Peanut Crumble (page 120)

Shredded BBQ Cabbage (page 127)

Cut the tempeh blocks into ¾-inch (2-cm) fingers.

To create the marinade, combine the red wine, tamari, peanut oil, smooth peanut butter and chili flakes in a closed container. Place the tempeh fingers inside. Marinate them overnight, or for at least 4 hours, before proceeding with the recipe.

In the meantime, prepare your sauce. In a small bowl, whisk together the smooth peanut butter, tamari, apple cider vinegar, tomato paste, chili flakes, cornstarch and water until smooth.

Preheat your oven to 375°F (190°C). Line a baking sheet with parchment paper.

Carefully remove the tempeh fingers from the marinade and dip each finger into the peanut sauce. Allow for any excess to drop off, then generously coat the tempeh fingers in sesame seeds and place them on the baking sheet. Reserve the remaining peanut sauce.

Roast the tempeh in the oven for 20 to 30 minutes, or until golden and crispy. In the meantime, whisk and heat the sauce on the stove over low heat for 5 to 10 minutes to thicken.

Remove the tempeh fingers from the oven and serve them drizzled in the remaining peanut sauce. They are fantastic served alongside parsnip mash or the sweet potato–peanut crumble and BBQ cabbage.

SEITAN SHOWSTOPPERS

The seitan recipes in this chapter are true showstoppers. The Sunday Seitan Schnitzel (page 81) is an homage to my home country, and I've also included classics such as Meatloaf-Style Seitan (page 64), Smoky Jackfruit Seitan Brisket (page 75) and Cranberry-Stuffed Turkey-Style Roast (page 67). And I've created new flavor excursions such as succulent Roasted Red Pepper Chick'n (page 79). Once you've come to love seitan, you'll never look back!

If you've never made seitan from scratch, don't you worry: I've got you covered! I've included an introduction to seitan on page 156, showing you the techniques I used in these recipes in more detail. I've included some easy troubleshooting, so you can get into the kitchen and get creative with seitan yourself or follow the step-by-step recipes in this chapter.

I love experimenting in the kitchen, and making seitan from scratch gives you so much control over the aromas and textures. And I've loved creating each and every showstopper recipe for you! Some of my favorites are the Teriyaki Seitan Steak (page 91), the Braised Red Wine Roast (page 73) and the Slow-Roasted Mustard Chick'n (page 69), which I'm sure will get your mouth watering.

Now off to the kitchen to create a delicious feast for friends and family—and yourself, of course!

MEATLOAF-STYLE SEITAN

I would do anything for roast . . . okay, let's stop here with the Meat Loaf references—which you will probably only understand if you're at least my age. This Meatloaf-Style Seitan is super easy to make; all you need is a blender or food processor and a loaf pan, and you're basically ready to go! It's created with tomato ketchup and chopped tomatoes to give it that juicy, chunky and light texture you know from classic meatloaf. It's a delicious crowd-pleaser for your next feast!

Serves 4 to 6

For the Seitan

2 cups (280 g) vital wheat gluten

½ cup (40 g) nutritional yeast

1 tsp garlic powder

2 tsp (5 g) onion powder

1 tsp sweet paprika

½ tsp ground cumin

½ tsp dried sage

½ tsp dried oregano

½ tsp sea salt

¼ tsp ground black pepper

⅓ cup (80 ml) ketchup, plus 2–3 tbsp (35–70 ml) for the coating

½ cup (90 g) chopped tomatoes

1 tsp hot sauce

2 tbsp (30 ml) tamari

¾ cup (185 ml) vegetable stock

Parsley, for garnish (optional)

For Serving

Shredded BBQ Cabbage (page 127)

Crunchy Rutabaga Fingers (page 128)

Stuffed Tomatoes (page 132)

Roasted Red Pepper Gravy (page 144)

Also: anything, but not THAT

Preheat your oven to 325°F (162°C).

In a large bowl, combine the vital wheat gluten, nutritional yeast, garlic powder, onion powder, paprika, cumin, dried sage, dried oregano, salt and black pepper. In a blender, combine the ketchup, tomatoes, hot sauce, tamari and vegetable stock.

Slowly add the dry mixture to the blender, while pulsing every 2 to 3 seconds. Process until all the ingredients are combined. It should result in a sticky, but loose seitan mixture.

Line an 8 x 4–inch (20 x 10–cm) loaf pan with aluminum foil, then line it with parchment paper. Transfer the seitan mixture to the loaf pan and wrap the excess parchment and aluminum foil over the top of the seitan.

Bake the mixture for 60 minutes. Carefully unwrap the foil and brush the seitan meatloaf with ketchup. Roast, uncovered, for 15 to 20 minutes, or until the top of the seitan is golden.

Remove the seitan from the loaf pan, garnishing it with the parsley, if desired, then slice and serve immediately. It will also keep for up to 3 days in the fridge in an airtight container.

Enjoy this vegan meatloaf alongside BBQ cabbage, rutabaga fingers and stuffed tomatoes. Drizzle with roasted red pepper gravy—yum!

CRANBERRY-STUFFED TURKEY-STYLE ROAST

This is the perfect dinner table addition for the next celebratory occasion, such as Christmas or Thanksgiving! It has the perfect festive touch with its sweet, zesty cranberry filling combined with the fruity glaze. The lightly crunchy outer layer is made from soymilk skin—also called yuba! It's simply divine served alongside roast potatoes, Yorkies and miso mash. Make your ultimate festive meal complete with a red wine gravy or the lemon mustard sauce.

Serves 8

For the Roast

2 cups (280 g) vital wheat gluten

½ cup (60 g) chickpea flour (gram flour)

¼ cup (20 g) nutritional yeast

½ tsp white pepper

2 tsp (5 g) onion powder

½ tsp garlic powder

1 tbsp (16 g) vegan poultry seasoning

1 (7-oz [200-g]) block extra-firm tofu

1 (15-oz [425-g]) can unsalted, organic chickpeas (with the liquid)

½ cup (125 ml) water

2 tbsp (30 ml) tamari

1 tbsp (15 ml) olive oil

For the Cranberry Filling

1½ cups (150 g) cranberries

1 tbsp (14 g) light brown sugar, packed

In a large mixing bowl, combine the vital wheat gluten, chickpea flour, nutritional yeast, white pepper, onion powder, garlic powder and poultry seasoning.

To a food processor, add the tofu, chickpeas (including the liquid!), water, tamari and olive oil. Process for 1 to 2 minutes, or until the mixture is smooth. If needed, stop the processor and scrape down the sides with a spatula until everything is blended nicely.

Add the wet mixture into the bowl and combine with the dry ingredients using a spatula or wooden spoon. Once it gets too sticky to combine with the spatula or spoon, switch to using your hands and knead the dough in the bowl until thoroughly combined. Keep your hands lightly oiled for easier kneading. Alternatively, you can knead everything together in a stand mixer with a dough hook attachment until well combined. Set the dough ball in a bowl and set it aside for 30 minutes.

In the meantime, place the cranberries and brown sugar in a small saucepan over medium heat and cook for 10 to 15 minutes, stirring frequently. Once the cranberries begin to soften, squish them with the back of a spoon to break them down and stir them in with the melting brown sugar. You should end up with a thick cranberry sauce. If it's still too watery, simmer it over low heat. If it's too dry, add a little water at a time, until you get your preferred texture.

Preheat your oven to 390°F (200°C). Place a rack in the middle and place an ovenproof dish filled with 70 to 105 ounces (2 to 3 L) of water in the bottom of your oven.

(continued)

For the Coating

1¼ cups (300 ml) soymilk

2 tbsp (28 g) unsalted vegan butter

1 tbsp (15 ml) olive oil

1 tsp maple syrup

1 tbsp (2 g) chopped fresh rosemary

1 tbsp (2 g) chopped fresh sage leaves

1 tbsp (15 ml) fresh lemon juice

½ tsp lemon zest

¼ tsp sweet paprika

½ tsp sea salt

For Serving

The Perfect Roast Potatoes (page 104)

Vegan Yorkies (page 108)

Parsnip and Miso Mash (page 124)

Red Wine Gravy (page 136) or Lemon Mustard Sauce (page 143)

On a piece of parchment paper, roll out the seitan mixture to a rectangle of roughly 8 x 12 inches (20 x 30 cm), and spread the cranberry sauce across, leaving about ½ inch (1 cm) empty around the edges. Starting on the long edge, roll up the seitan—with the cranberry sauce on the inside—into a large log. Pinch and twist the ends to seal, then firmly wrap the roast in parchment, followed by two to three layers of tightly wrapped strong aluminum foil.

Place the wrapped seitan in an ovenproof dish and place it in the middle of the oven. Roast at 390°F (200°C) for 1 hour, then carefully remove the roast from the oven and remove the wrapping.

Ten minutes before the end of the roasting process, prepare the coating for the turkey roast.

Pour the soymilk in a wide nonstick skillet and bring it to a simmer over medium-low heat. Allow it to simmer for 1 to 2 minutes, until a skin begins to form on the top of the milk. Once it starts appearing, simmer for 3 to 4 minutes to thicken the skin. Using a ladle or spatula, carefully lift the soymilk skin off the liquid and place it on the seitan log to wrap. Repeat until you have enough skin to cover the entire log.

While your milk is simmering away, combine the vegan butter, olive oil, maple syrup, rosemary, sage, lemon juice, zest, paprika and salt in a small saucepan over low heat. Stir all the ingredients together until the butter is melted and the seasoning is well combined.

Brush the seasoning mixture over the entire skin-covered log. Place it back into the oven to roast for 15 to 20 minutes, or until the skin is lightly crispy on the outside. Remove the roast from the oven and slice it up!

This festive roast is fantastic served alongside roast potatoes, Yorkies and mash. It works well with a variety of sauces. I'd recommend the red wine gravy or the lemon mustard sauce, which works wonderfully alongside the seasoning of this seitan roast. Time to tuck in!

SLOW-ROASTED MUSTARD CHICK'N

Good things take time, just like this Slow-Roasted Mustard Chick'n! What I love most about slow-roasted seitan recipes is how wonderfully the seitan takes on the flavors and how tender it comes out. This recipe has a succulent, chicken-like texture and a delicious sweetness that works perfectly with the mellow yet sharp notes of the Dijon mustard glaze. You can roast this dish ahead of time, then keep it in the fridge for up to 3 days. On the day of serving, add the mustard glaze, roast for 25 to 30 minutes and you're all set!

Serves 6 to 8

For the Seitan

12.3 oz (350 g) silken tofu

1 (14-oz [400-g]) can chickpeas in unsalted water, with the liquid

2 tbsp (30 ml) vegetable oil

1 tbsp (16 g) white miso paste

1 (0.4-oz [11-g]) cube vegetable bouillon

½ tsp baking powder

2 tsp (10 g) vegan poultry seasoning

¼ tsp garlic powder

½ tsp onion powder

2¼ cups (315 g) vital wheat gluten

For the Broth

½ cup (50 g) vegan poultry seasoning

6 cups (1.4 L) water

1 tsp onion powder

Handful of fresh herbs, such as thyme, sage and rosemary

6 cloves garlic

Add the silken tofu, chickpeas, oil, white miso paste, bouillon cube, baking powder, poultry seasoning, garlic powder and onion powder to a high-speed blender or food processor. Blend for 5 minutes until smooth.

If your processor has a dough hook, switch to it and sprinkle in the vital wheat gluten. Alternatively, transfer the blended mixture to a large bowl and stir in the vital wheat gluten with a wooden spoon or spatula. Switch to using your hands, once the mixture becomes too difficult to combine with a spoon or spatula. Combine everything into a firm dough and place it in a bowl to rest for 1 hour.

Preheat your oven to 300°F (150°C).

For this section, refer to the photos on the next page. On parchment paper, roll and stretch out the seitan dough into a long, thin log. It doesn't need to be a specific width or length, just long enough for you to knot it without it ripping. Make a knot in the dough, then press it flat with your hands or a rolling pin and stretch it out again. Repeat 3 to 4 times until you have made multiple firm knots in the dough. Place the seitan back in the bowl to rest while you prepare the simmering broth.

In a large bowl combine the poultry seasoning, water, onion powder, fresh herbs and garlic. Add the broth to a casserole dish and place the knotted seitan inside, so it's just about covered by the liquid. Cover with a lid or aluminum foil and roast for 2 hours. Do not open the oven door. When the 2 hours elapse, allow the roast to cool in the oven for at least 1 hour. If you're making this seitan ahead of time, transfer the entire casserole dish to the fridge and you can keep it there for up to 3 days.

(continued)

For the Mustard Glaze

2 tbsp (30 ml) Dijon mustard

1 tbsp (15 ml) maple syrup

1 tsp crushed garlic

1 tbsp (15 ml) fresh lemon juice

1 tbsp (3 g) dried thyme

For Serving

The Perfect Roast Potatoes (page 104) or Parsnip and Miso Mash (page 124)

Roasted Sprouts with Smoky Tofu Bits (page 123)

Pecan and Apple Stuffing (page 107)

While the seitan cools, prepare the glaze: In a medium-sized bowl, whisk together the Dijon mustard, maple syrup, crushed garlic, lemon juice and dried thyme.

Remove the seitan from the broth and place it into an ovenproof dish, then increase your oven temperature to 390°F (200°C). Brush it generously with the glaze, then transfer it to the oven uncovered to roast for 25 to 30 minutes. Halfway through, carefully remove it from the oven and brush it with another layer of glaze before returning it to the oven.

Once the roasting time finishes, it should be golden and ready to serve. Drizzle it with any leftover glaze and slice it into six to eight portions. It's best served alongside roast potatoes or parsnip mash and delicious with roasted sprouts and stuffing.

BRAISED RED WINE ROAST

With its deep, mellow notes of red wine, this braised seitan roast is truly a special treat! It's one of the quicker seitan recipes you will find in this book, and it gets its wonderful flavor notes from red wine, cinnamon and ginger. The simple texture comes from frying and simmering this roast. It's one of the easiest ways to make delicious seitan, if you ask me. And without any long resting times, I had to include this recipe for you as a great option for last-minute feasts!

What I love about this recipe is that the seitan turns out wonderfully juicy and soft. It pairs perfectly with a hearty red wine gravy, roast potatoes, Yorkies and roasted cabbage on the side!

Serves 4 to 6

For the Seitan

3 cups (420 g) vital wheat gluten

¼ cup (43 g) all-purpose flour

1 tbsp (7 g) onion powder

1 tsp garlic powder

1 tbsp (8 g) porcini mushroom powder

1 tbsp (7 g) nutritional yeast

½ tsp ground black pepper

½ tsp ground cinnamon

¼ tsp ginger powder

1 tbsp (15 ml) red wine vinegar

1¾ cups (435 ml) red wine

2 tbsp (30 ml) tamari

1-inch (2.5-cm) red food coloring gel (optional)

In a large mixing bowl, combine the vital wheat gluten, flour, onion powder, garlic powder, porcini mushroom powder, nutritional yeast, black pepper, cinnamon and ginger powder. Set it aside. In a large bowl, combine the red wine vinegar, red wine and tamari. Whisk in the red food coloring gel. If you're using food coloring, wear gloves when handling it. I highly recommend it to get a wonderful color.

Pour the wet mixture into the bowl with the dry ingredients. Knead them together for 4 to 5 minutes into a smooth dough ball. Set it aside to rest for 30 minutes for the gluten to activate.

(continued)

For the Panfry and Braising Process

2 tbsp (30 ml) olive oil

2 tbsp (30 ml) tamari

1 cup (240 ml) red wine, divided

1 tsp black peppercorns

2 cinnamon sticks

1 (1-inch [2.5-cm]) piece sliced fresh ginger

2 cups (473 ml) vegetable stock

For Serving

Red Wine Gravy (page 136)

The Perfect Roast Potatoes (page 104)

Vegan Yorkies (page 108)

Roasted Cabbage Steaks (page 42)

Heat the olive oil in a large, nonstick skillet with a lid. Fry the roast on each side for 3 to 4 minutes, until a lightly crispy skin forms. Pour the tamari and ½ cup (125 ml) of red wine into the open pan and cook for 8 to 10 minutes, or until the wine has reduced and caramelized. Flip the roast about once a minute to prevent it from sticking to the pan. In the meantime, preheat your oven to 390°F (200°C).

Transfer the seitan to an ovenproof dish with the peppercorns, cinnamon sticks and ginger. Pour in the rest of the red wine and vegetable stock, and cover the dish with aluminum foil.

Transfer it to the oven and roast for 25 to 30 minutes. The roast will expand to about twice its original size during this cooking process. Allow the roast to rest in the oven for at least 30 minutes after the roasting for the seitan texture to settle. Then it's ready to serve!

This Braised Red Wine Roast is delicious served with—you guessed it—red wine gravy, with a side of roast potatoes, Yorkies and roasted cabbage steaks!

SMOKY JACKFRUIT SEITAN BRISKET

This brisket is soft on the inside, with a meaty fried crust, and it's roasted in a smoky and salty glaze. Welcome to roast heaven! This dish will make you feel right at home at a backyard barbecue. I love making this seitan brisket with potato mash, cabbage and corn bread dumplings, with some crunchy Yorkies on the side. The best sauces to pair this brisket with are the roasted red pepper and the red wine gravy.

Prepare this ahead of time by transferring the brisket and broth to an airtight container after simmering and storing it in the fridge for up to three days. On the glorious day of serving this brisket, drain, panfry and roast it in the oven along with the remaining ingredients.

Serves 4 to 6

For the Seitan

2 cups (280 g) vital wheat gluten

2 tbsp (12 g) mushroom powder

1 tsp sea salt

½ cup (40 g) nutritional yeast

½ tsp cocoa powder

1 (8.5-oz [240-g]) can black beans, drained

1 tbsp (15 ml) liquid smoke

1 tbsp (15 ml) balsamic vinegar

2 tbsp (30 ml) ketchup

1 tbsp (15 g) brown miso paste

3 tsp (15 g) crushed garlic

1 tbsp (15 ml) olive oil

1 tbsp (15 ml) tamari

¾-inch (2-cm) red food coloring gel (optional)

1 (7.4-oz [210-g]) can shredded jackfruit, drained and with the seeds removed

2–3 tbsp (28–42 ml) olive oil, for frying

2 tbsp (32 g) tomato paste

1 tbsp (15 ml) maple syrup

¼ tsp smoked paprika

1 tbsp (15 ml) tamari

In a large mixing bowl, combine the vital wheat gluten, mushroom powder, salt, nutritional yeast and cocoa powder. Set it aside. In a food processor, blend the drained black beans, liquid smoke, balsamic vinegar, ketchup, miso paste, garlic, oil, tamari and red food coloring (if using). Be sure to wear gloves! I always love my brisket in a delicious pink color, so I definitely recommend adding some color to the mix!

Blend until everything is smoothly combined, then shred the drained jackfruit with your hands into the dry ingredients and pour in the blended mixture right after. Use a spatula or wooden spoon to combine everything into a dough ball. Once it gets too difficult to combine, switch to using your hands and knead the dough in the bowl for 2 to 3 minutes. Form it into a ball and allow it to rest in the bowl for 30 minutes.

(continued)

For the Broth

2 (0.4-oz [11-g]) cubes vegetable bouillon

1 cup (240 ml) vegan red wine

1 tbsp (15 ml) olive oil

2 tbsp (30 ml) tamari

1 tsp liquid smoke

½ tsp smoked paprika

For Serving

Roasted Red Pepper Gravy (page 144) or Red Wine Gravy (page 136)

Ranch Potato Mash (page 115)

Vegan Yorkies (page 108)

Shredded BBQ Cabbage (page 127)

Chilli Cheeze Corn Bread Dumplings (page 116)

In the meantime, prepare the simmering broth: In a large, lidded saucepan combine the bouillon cubes, red wine, olive oil, tamari, liquid smoke and smoked paprika. Heat over low heat and stir until the bouillon cubes are dissolved.

Place the seitan into the simmering broth, cover the saucepan with a lid and simmer for 30 to 40 minutes over low heat, flipping the seitan halfway through. Once done, allow the seitan brisket to cool in the broth for 45 minutes. If you're making this recipe ahead of time, transfer the cooled seitan and broth to an airtight container and keep it in the fridge for up to 3 days.

Preheat your oven to 390°F (200°C).

Remove the seitan brisket from the simmering broth and place it in a colander for 10 to 15 minutes for any excess liquid to drip off.

Heat the oil in a large, nonstick pan over medium heat. Fry the bottom of the brisket for 8 to 10 minutes, or until a lightly crispy layer forms at the bottom. Flip and fry for 4 to 5 minutes on the second side.

Transfer the brisket to an ovenproof dish. In a small bowl, combine the tomato paste, maple syrup, smoked paprika and tamari. Brush the mixture over the top of the brisket and roast it in the oven for 20 to 25 minutes.

To serve, move the brisket to a serving platter and slice into four to six portions. I love serving this seitan brisket drizzled with roasted red pepper or red wine gravy alongside potato mash, Yorkies, roasted cabbage and corn bread dumplings.

ROASTED RED PEPPER CHICK'N

This vibrant recipe was actually the result of a delicious experiment! To be honest, the best recipes come from spontaneous kitchen experiments, and this one is definitely a gem. The light and soft seitan for this Roasted Red Pepper Chick'n is created in two batches to create two chick'n-style roasts. They are the perfect size to easily portion and share on the feasting table! The roast is coated in a thin soymilk skin that is called yuba. It becomes beautifully crispy in the oven and teams up wonderfully with the roasted, smoky flavors of the homemade roasted red pepper sauce!

Serves 4 to 6

For the Seitan

16 cups (1.1 kg) strong white bread flour, divided

3 cups (710 ml) water, divided

2 tbsp (32 g) vegan poultry seasoning, divided

2 tsp (5 g) onion powder, divided

1¼ cups (300 ml) soymilk

4–5 fresh lemon slices (optional)

For the Sauce

1 cup (225 g) roughly chopped red bell pepper

¾ cup (120 g) roughly chopped red onion

3 cloves garlic, roasted and peeled

½–1 tbsp (7–14 ml) olive oil

½ tsp ground black pepper

½ tsp sea salt

½ tsp chili flakes

1 cup (240 ml) dairy-free cream

1 (0.4-oz [11-g]) cube vegetable bouillon

In two separate mixing bowls, combine half of the flour and half of the water per bowl. Use a spoon to form each into a dough ball. Knead each one on a lightly floured surface for 5 minutes, then return to each bowl and add enough water to cover. Allow the dough balls to soak for at least 30 minutes, then knead the dough balls underwater to release their starches. Drain the water after 5 minutes, fill up again and repeat the process until the water no longer turns thick and white, but only a little cloudy. It should take about eight to ten washing cycles until you get there. The washed flour should feel loose and stringy once the majority of starch is washed out.

Rest each washed dough ball separately in a colander or a cheesecloth-lined sieve in the fridge for at least 4 hours or ideally overnight.

Transfer one seitan dough ball at a time to a food processor, add half the poultry seasoning and onion powder to each and pulse the processor for 1 minute to incorporate the seasoning. Squeeze each dough ball between your hands to roughly shape and make it come back together, then rest it in a fine-mesh sieve for 30 minutes.

Roll out each dough ball on a dry cutting board and stretch it into a long strand of roughly 12 inches (30 cm) length. Knot each strand three to four times, until the dough comes together into a firm little parcel, then let it rest for at least 20 minutes.

Gently flatten each seitan knot with the palms of your hands, then tightly wrap each knotted ball in three to four layers of strong aluminum foil and steam in a steaming basket for 30 to 40 minutes. Allow the seitan to cool for 15 minutes before removing it from the foil.

(continued)

ROASTED RED PEPPER CHICK'N (CONTINUED)

For Serving

The Perfect Roast Potatoes
(page 104)

Shredded BBQ Cabbage
(page 127)

Stuffed Tomatoes (page 132)

Ranch Potato Mash (page 115)

In the meantime, preheat your oven to 400°F (204°C). To make the sauce, drizzle your red bell pepper, onion and garlic with olive oil and roast them for 20 to 25 minutes, or until soft and the edges of the peppers are lightly browned. Then transfer to a blender and process until smooth. Stir the black pepper, salt, chili flakes, dairy-free cream and bouillon cube into the red pepper sauce.

Heat the soymilk over medium-low heat in a wide pan for 10 to 15 minutes, until the milk skin begins to form on top. Once it starts appearing, wait for 5 minutes for the skin to get a little thicker; don't stir in the meantime. Using a spatula, carefully lift the soymilk skin off the pan and carefully wrap the first seitan ball in the skin. Continue to cook the milk until skin forms again. Let it thicken for 5 minutes, then carefully lift it off and wrap it around the seitan. Repeat until both seitan balls are wrapped completely in about two layers of skin.

Lifting the skin and wrapping might require a little practice, so don't worry if it's not 100 percent perfect the first time around. It will be worth it as this forms the crispy chick'n skin on the seitan and becomes wonderfully crispy in the oven.

While you're doing this, preheat your oven to 400°F (204°C).

Transfer the blended red pepper sauce to an ovenproof dish. Place the skin-wrapped seitan parcels in the sauce and gently brush a little of the sauce onto each parcel. They should not be fully submerged in the sauce but peek out.

Place 1 slice of lemon (if using) onto each piece and add the rest of the slices to the sauce. Roast for 25 to 30 minutes, or until the sauce has thickened and the chick'n pieces have gotten wonderfully golden and crispy on top.

To serve, carefully remove the seitan from the dish, remove the lemon and gently cut each chick'n piece into slices. Serve with the remainder of the sauce. These Roasted Red Pepper Chick'n pieces are simply delicious on their own, but also perfect with roast potatoes, BBQ cabbage, stuffed tomatoes and potato mash.

SUNDAY SEITAN SCHNITZEL

Whenever I tell people I grew up in Germany, they ask me if I ate a lot of schnitzel growing up. True story! It's one of the traditional and best-known meals served in my home country, so of course I had to include a delicious veganized schnitzel recipe in this book. This one is inspired by a traditional chick'n schnitzel. This recipe makes two large schnitzels, which are a great size to serve with potatoes and some simple steamed veg.

Serves 2

For the Seitan

3 cups (455 g) strong white bread flour (minimum 14% protein)

1⅓ cups (311 ml) water

1 tbsp (15 g) powder from crumbled vegetable bouillon cubes

1 tbsp plus 1 tsp (20 g) vegan poultry seasoning

2–3 tbsp (30–45 ml) vegetable oil

For the Broth

8 cups (1.9 L) water

2 tbsp (32 g) vegan poultry seasoning

2 (0.4-oz [11-g]) cubes vegetable bouillon

1 tbsp (15 ml) apple cider vinegar

2 tsp (10 ml) white miso paste

For the Coating

⅔ cup (105 g) chickpea flour (gram flour)

⅛ tsp black salt (kala namak) for an extra 'eggy' flavor (optional)

⅛ tsp ground black pepper

1 cup plus 1 tbsp (252 ml) soymilk

¾ cup (90 g) breadcrumbs

½ tsp smoked paprika

Combine the flour and water into a firm dough ball. Knead it for 2 minutes, then set it in a bowl to rest for 1 hour.

Fill the bowl with water to fully submerge the dough ball underwater and allow it to rest for 30 minutes. Then knead the dough ball underwater to release the wheat starches from the dough.

Once the water around the dough is thickening and white, drain and refill the bowl with fresh water. Repeat four to five times until the water is lighter and the majority of the starch is washed out. Place the ball in a colander and rinse one final time. The remaining gluten ball should be very loose and almost falling apart. Don't worry; this is exactly what we are looking for and the dough will come back together in the next step.

Sprinkle the crumbled bouillon powder and poultry seasoning onto the gluten ball and fold it in with your hands until evenly distributed. Allow the gluten to rest in the colander at room temperature for at least 1 hour or overnight in the fridge, so the gluten can activate and come back together to form a tight ball.

Once the resting time elapses, give the dough ball a good knead between your hands and divide it into two parts. Roughly shape it into your desired schnitzel shape: Press the seitan ball into a flat shape using your hands or a rolling pin to ½ inch (1 cm) thick as it will expand in the next step.

In a large saucepan, combine the water, poultry seasoning, vegetable bouillon cubes, apple cider vinegar and white miso paste and bring it to a boil over medium heat. Reduce the heat to low and place both schnitzels in the broth. Allow them to simmer for 45 minutes. Turn off the heat and let the seitan cool in the broth; this should take about 1 hour.

(continued)

For Serving

The Perfect Roast Potatoes
(page 104)

Smoky Crusted Green Beans
(page 131)

Crunchy Rutabaga Fingers
(page 128) or Ranch Potato
Mash (page 115)

Your favorite gravy

If you're making these ahead of time, you can transfer the dough pieces to two freezer bags, spoon about 1 cup (240 ml) of broth into each bag and rest them in the fridge for up to 10 days.

Remove each schnitzel from the broth and press each schnitzel on a cutting board until they are about ½ inch (1 cm) thick. Allow them to rest for 5 minutes while you create the coating and breading.

In a shallow bowl, combine the chickpea flour, black salt (if using), black pepper and soymilk. Whisk together until smooth. In a shallow plate, place the breadcrumbs and smoked paprika seasoning.

You can keep the schnitzels in the oven at 300°F (150°C) for up to 1 hour until the rest of your roast is ready to serve. To prepare them: Heat the vegetable oil in a large, nonstick skillet. Place each schnitzel into the smooth batter until evenly coated. Allow any excess to drip off, then coat each schnitzel in the breadcrumb mixture. Fry them in the hot oil for 5 to 6 minutes, flipping halfway through, until golden on both sides. Transfer the schnitzels onto a kitchen towel to remove any excess oil.

Traditionally, this schnitzel is served with boiled potatoes and steamed veg and drizzled in fresh lemon juice. You can also pair it with roast potatoes, crusted green beans, rutabaga fingers or ranch mash and a drizzle of your favorite gravy.

GERMAN-STYLE POT ROAST

Pot roast used to be a regular guest on the dinner table when I was growing up. I vividly remember my mum preparing the roast in the morning and it sizzling away in the oven for a couple of hours before it was served with potatoes and veg. This vegan version of a German-style pot roast is loaded with umami flavor and gives home-cooked comfort food a whole new meaning. It has a soft and succulent texture and is slow roasted in the oven, giving it the ultimate depth of satisfying flavors.

To prepare this recipe ahead of time, stop after the flour washing process and rest your dough ball in a colander in the fridge. You can hold it there for up to 3 days before incorporating the seasoning and roasting this bad boy.

Serves 8

For the Seitan

8 cups (1.1 kg) strong white bread flour (minimum 12% protein)

24 oz (720 ml) water

3 tbsp (45 ml) vegetable oil

2 tbsp (40 g) tomato paste

1 tbsp (15 ml) balsamic vinegar

2 tbsp (30 ml) tamari

¼ cup (60 ml) vegan red wine

Divide the flour and water, mixing half of each in two separate mixing bowls. This makes the seitan easier to handle throughout the process. If you own a humongous mixing bowl, feel free to mix it all at once.

Knead the two dough balls on a lightly floured surface until smooth. Set them aside to rest for 30 minutes. During this time the gluten will develop.

Completely submerge each dough ball in water in its bowl and allow it to soak for at least 30 minutes, then knead and squish each dough ball between your hands under the water to wash it. This will release the starches from the flour, which are soluble in the water.

Do the first wash for 5 minutes; during this time the water will become white and slightly thicken. Drain the water, refill with fresh water and wash for 2 minutes. Drain again, refill and wash once more for 1 minute. The dough should become soft, stringy and spongy; it will feel like it is almost falling apart and the water will be much clearer than during the first wash, but not quite clear. We want to remove a decent amount of starch—but not all of it—to get the right texture for this recipe. It takes a little bit of experimenting and also the use of the right flour to get this right to your preference.

Once both dough balls have been washed, add them both together to a colander and squish them together gently. Rinse with water for 20 seconds, then set it aside to drain and rest in the colander.

(continued)

For the Seitan Seasoning

2 tbsp (10 g) nutritional yeast

2 tbsp (30 g) chickpea flour (gram flour)

1 tsp dried sage

1 tsp onion powder

½ tsp garlic powder

¼ tsp red food coloring gel (optional)

For the Roasting Stock Mix

½ cup (125 ml) coffee

2 cups (473 ml) vegan red wine

2 tbsp (30 ml) balsamic vinegar

2 tbsp (32 g) tomato paste

1 tbsp (15 ml) Dijon mustard

3 tbsp (45 ml) tamari

1 tbsp (15 ml) maple syrup

2–3 tbsp (10–15 g) mixed fresh herbs, such as thyme, sage or rosemary

2–3 cups (473–710 ml) vegetable stock

25 oz (709 g) mixed vegetables (I like to use carrots, potato, red onion, celery and mushrooms)

2 bay leaves

1 tbsp (8 g) cornstarch

2 tbsp (30 ml) water

For Serving

The Perfect Roast Potatoes (page 104)

Vegan Yorkies (page 108)

In this process, the loose, soft gluten dough will come back together and thicken; this will determine the texture in the final pot roast. Ideally, allow the dough to rest overnight for best results. If you're in a rush, give it at least 1 hour. If you are making this recipe in advance, you can prepare the dough up to 3 days in advance, cover it, place the colander in a bowl and set it in the fridge.

Next, it's time to season the seitan! Combine the nutritional yeast, chickpea flour, dried sage, onion powder and garlic powder in a small bowl. Remove the gluten dough from the colander and knead it on a wet kitchen surface. Sprinkle the seasoning mix onto the gluten while you're kneading it to distribute it throughout the dough. Alternatively, you can use a stand mixer with a dough hook to knead the dough and incorporate the spices. If you want your seitan to have a vibrant and meat-like red coloring, you can incorporate red food coloring gel in this process and knead it into the dough until well combined. Be sure to wear gloves!

Sear the seitan to give it a delicious crust: Heat the vegetable oil in a large, nonstick skillet over high heat and place the seitan inside. Fry on each side for 2 minutes, then reduce the heat to low. Add the tomato paste, balsamic vinegar, tamari and red wine to the pan and allow the seitan to simmer for 10 minutes. This process will incorporate any remaining liquid into the seitan and also help firm up the shape, making it ready for the roasting process.

Preheat your oven to 340°F (171°C).

To a large casserole dish with a lid, add the roasting stock mixture: coffee, red wine, balsamic vinegar, tomato paste, mustard, tamari, maple syrup, fresh herbs, vegetable stock, mixed vegetables and bay leaves. Place the seitan in the roasting stock, gently pressing it down so it's just about covered in the liquid. Cover the casserole dish with the lid.

Transfer it to the preheated oven and roast for 2 hours. Remove the lid and roast for 1 hour uncovered.

To serve, remove the seitan roast from the stock and slice into 1-inch (2.5-cm) pieces. Strain the stock to remove the large veg pieces and heat the remaining liquid in a saucepan. Mix the cornstarch with 2 tablespoons (30 ml) of water to create a slurry. Stir it into the stock to thicken it and turn it into a delicious gravy to serve alongside. Remove it from the heat after roughly 2 to 3 minutes, or once it gets to your desired consistency. Enjoy with some delicious roast potatoes and Yorkies!

ORANGE-GLAZED SEITAN HAM

This seitan ham recipe will amaze you! It's wonderfully salty and smoky, and it's roasted to perfection with a fruity and zesty orange glaze. It's perfect to serve for your next family feast, and any leftovers are perfect to thinly slice and serve in a delicious vegan ham sandwich!

Serves 4 to 6

For the Seitan

3 cups (405 g) vital wheat gluten

½ cup (48 g) chickpea flour (gram flour)

¼ cup (15 g) nutritional yeast

2 tsp (5 g) onion powder

1 tsp garlic powder

1 tsp smoked paprika

1 tsp ground black pepper

¼ tsp ground cloves

¼ cup (60 ml) fresh orange juice (roughly ½ medium orange)

¼ cup (60 ml) tamari

2 tbsp (30 ml) maple syrup

2 tbsp (30 ml) liquid smoke

1 (0.4-oz [11-g]) cube vegetable bouillon

1 cup (240 ml) water

1-inch (2.5-cm) red food coloring gel (optional)

20–30 whole cloves

In a large bowl, combine the vital wheat gluten, chickpea flour, nutritional yeast, onion powder, garlic powder, smoked paprika, black pepper and ground cloves.

In a separate bowl, combine the orange juice, tamari, maple syrup, liquid smoke, bouillon cube and water. If you're looking for a delicious pink coloring in your seitan ham, also stir in the red food coloring gel. If using, be sure to wear gloves! Whisk everything together until the bouillon cube is fully dissolved.

Pour the wet ingredients into the dry and knead everything into a dough ball, then dust a surface with a little extra vital wheat gluten and knead the dough by hand for 10 minutes to develop the gluten. You should get a smooth dough with individual gluten strands visible on the top. Place the dough ball in a bowl and set it aside to rest for 30 minutes.

In the meantime, preheat your oven to 380°F (193°C) and place a rack in the middle. Pour 70 to 105 ounces (2–3 L) of water into an ovenproof dish and place it in the bottom of your oven.

Once the resting time elapses, cover the seitan in one layer of parchment paper, then tightly wrap it in three to four layers of heavy-duty aluminum foil. Steam it in the oven for 45 minutes, turning it halfway through. Once done, turn off the oven and allow the seitan to sit in the oven for at least 2 hours to cool completely.

(continued)

For the Glaze

4 tbsp (56 g) vegan butter

1 tbsp (15 ml) Dijon mustard

2 tbsp (30 ml) fresh orange juice (roughly ¼ medium orange)

2 oz (54 ml) fresh lemon juice

2 tbsp (28 g) light brown sugar, packed

1 tbsp (16 ml) molasses

2 tbsp (30 ml) vegan brandy (optional)

For Serving

Red Wine Gravy (page 136)

The Perfect Roast Potatoes (page 104)

Smoky Crusted Green Beans (page 131) or Roasted Sprouts with Smoky Tofu Bits (page 123)

In the meantime, prepare your glaze: In a small saucepan, melt the vegan butter, then stir in the Dijon mustard, orange juice, lemon juice, brown sugar, molasses and brandy (if using). Stir over low heat until all the ingredients are well combined, and the sugar is dissolved in the mixture, then remove it from the heat.

Preheat your oven to 380°F (193°C).

When your seitan is fully cooled down, carefully unwrap it. Use a small sharp knife to cut diagonal lines across the top of your seitan in a crisscross pattern. Transfer it to an ovenproof dish and stick 20 to 30 whole cloves into the top of the seitan. Brush half of the glaze across the seitan ham to evenly coat it, and bake for 20 minutes.

Carefully remove the roast from the oven, drizzle over the remaining liquid and return it to the hot oven for 5 minutes. Remove the roast from the oven, remove the whole cloves and thinly slice the seitan ham.

The ham slices are best enjoyed alongside a generous drizzle of red wine gravy, roast potatoes and green beans or sprouts.

TERIYAKI SEITAN STEAK

I personally never ate huge amounts of meat before going vegan, however steaks were some of the few things I thoroughly enjoyed. And to my surprise, it's actually not complicated to make a succulent and tender vegan steak. "Experimenting" is my middle name, and I enjoy testing out different flavors and techniques. This teriyaki seitan steak is one of my favorite ways to prepare a vegan steak! It is created with a base of strong white flour and uses the flour washing technique. It takes on the vibrant flavors of the seasoning and teriyaki sauce just beautifully! It's one of the quickest and easiest ways to use the flour washing method without extensively long resting times. It's perfect with miso parsnip mash, mushroom scallops and crusted green beans. Try it for yourself!

Serves 4

For the Seitan

8 cups (1.1 kg) strong white bread flour (minimum 12% protein)

2 cups (473 ml) water

3–4 drops red food coloring gel (optional)

1 tbsp (15 ml) sesame oil

For the Seasoning Mix

½ tsp ground black pepper

½ tsp onion powder

½ tsp sea salt

¼ tsp mustard powder

¼ tsp ground coriander seed

¼ tsp chili powder

⅛ tsp ground cumin

¼ tsp oregano

¼ tsp garlic powder

⅛ tsp ginger powder

1 (¼-inch [6-mm]) piece bay leaf, ground

In a large mixing bowl, combine the strong white bread flour and water, then knead it into a firm dough ball on a lightly floured surface. Set the dough ball back into the bowl and set it aside for 30 minutes. Once the time elapses, fill the bowl with fresh water to fully submerge the dough ball and set it aside for 20 minutes.

In the meantime, prepare the seasoning mix: Combine the black pepper, onion powder, salt, mustard powder, coriander, chili powder, cumin, oregano, garlic powder, ginger powder and ground bay leaf in a small bowl.

Place the bowl with the dough ball in your sink and knead and wash the dough underwater for 5 minutes to release the starches. Drain the water, refill with fresh water and repeat for two more times for 2 minutes each. Transfer the dough ball to a colander and rinse for 10 seconds. Set the colander aside and allow the dough to rest for at least 30 minutes in the colander. During this time the loose seitan ball will come back together, and its texture will firm up.

(continued)

For the Teriyaki Sauce

½ cup (125 ml) tamari

¼ cup (60 ml) maple syrup

¼ cup (60 ml) sake

2-inch (5-cm) piece fresh ginger, grated

2 tsp (10 g) minced garlic

½ tsp chili powder

1 tsp mirin

½ tsp toasted sesame oil

For Serving

Parsnip and Miso Mash (page 124)

Garlic Butter Mushroom Scallops (page 119)

Smoky Crusted Green Beans (page 131)

In the meantime, prepare your teriyaki sauce: In a medium-sized bowl, whisk together the tamari, maple syrup, sake, ginger, garlic, chili powder, mirin and toasted sesame oil.

Once the 30 minutes elapse, sprinkle the seasoning mix onto the gluten dough and knead it on a dry surface for a few minutes, until the seasoning is evenly distributed throughout the dough. If using, knead in the red food coloring gel—wear gloves! Divide the seitan into four roughly equal-sized pieces and roll each of them into an oval shape.

Preheat your oven to 375°F (190°C).

Heat the sesame oil in a large, nonstick skillet over medium heat, then place the seitan steaks into the hot oil. Fry on the first side for roughly 5 minutes, or until a light crust forms on the bottom. Flip and fry for 5 minutes on the second side. Gently press each seitan steak during the frying process to create a denser texture. I like to do this with a small saucepan and press it down with a hand wrapped in a kitchen towel.

Transfer the seitan steak to an ovenproof dish, pour the teriyaki sauce over the steak and transfer it to the oven to roast for 15 to 20 minutes. Serve each teriyaki steak alongside parsnip mash, mushroom scallops and green beans.

CRISPY CHICK'N-STYLE PANKO ROAST

This crispy panko roast reminds me very much of a crunchy, chicken-style schnitzel. However, instead of a thin, crunchy schnitzel-like layer, this seitan is thick and full of texture! The seitan dough is knotted to recreate a shredded poultry-like texture and a seasoned panko layer is added to the outside for an extra crunch. It's wonderful with roast potatoes, mushroom scallops, garlic and herb dip and roasted red pepper gravy. If you're prepping your panko roast ahead of time, keep it in the fridge after simmering for up to three days and add the crispy coating on the day of serving.

Serves 4 to 6

For the Seitan

8 cups (1.1 kg) strong white bread flour (minimum 12% protein)

2½ cups (600 ml) water

1 tbsp (7 g) onion powder

2 tbsp (32 g) vegan poultry seasoning

Combine the strong white bread flour and water in a medium-sized bowl. Knead the dough with your hands on a lightly floured surface for 10 minutes until the dough has created a firm and smooth dough ball. Set it aside to rest in the bowl for 20 minutes.

Once the time elapses, fill the bowl with water until the dough ball is completely submerged. Set it aside for 30 minutes, or up to 1 hour.

Start firmly kneading the dough with your hands underwater to release the wheat starch. Knead for 5 minutes, until the dough becomes lighter. The water should be white, thicker and cream-like. Drain the water, and fill the bowl with fresh water until the dough is submerged again. Knead for 2 minutes, then drain again. Repeat the refill, kneading and draining for two more times for 2 minutes each, then transfer the dough to a colander and rinse with water for 10 seconds. Set the dough and the colander aside to rest for at least 1 hour. During this time, the gluten strands will firm up and the loose dough ball will come back together.

Transfer the dough to a large, clean surface and knead and fold it. Sprinkle it with the onion powder and poultry seasoning. Knead it into the dough until well combined. Gently stretch it into a long log and pull it apart until it's long enough for you to knot it. I find roughly 12 inches (30 cm) is a good length to start the knotting! Once knotted, press the dough to flatten it slightly, stretch it into a log again and knot. Repeat four to five times. If you have any small loose strands on the sides, you can also knot them up. The knotting will help develop the chicken-like, shreddy texture. Try to knot it tightly without ripping the dough, but don't worry about being too neat.

(continued)

For the Roasting Stock

88 oz (2.5 L) vegetable stock

2 tbsp (32 g) vegan poultry seasoning

For the Coating

¼ cup (40 g) chickpea flour (gram flour)

1 tsp vegan poultry seasoning

½ tsp cayenne pepper, divided

½ cup (120 ml) plant milk

⅔ cup (70 g) panko breadcrumbs

½ tsp smoked paprika

For Serving

The Perfect Roast Potatoes (page 104)

Garlic Butter Mushroom Scallops (page 119)

Roasted Garlic and Herb White Bean Dip (page 151)

Roasted Red Pepper Gravy (page 144)

Once done, press the seitan into your desired shape and tightly wrap it in parchment paper, then cover it firmly with two to three layers of aluminum foil.

In a saucepan large enough for the seitan, heat the vegetable stock. Stir in the poultry seasoning, then add the wrapped seitan roast and simmer for 40 minutes. Allow it to cool in the stock for 30 minutes, then carefully remove it and unwrap it.

In the meantime, preheat your oven to 350°F (177°C). Line a baking sheet with parchment paper.

Whisk together the chickpea flour, poultry seasoning, ¼ teaspoon cayenne pepper and plant milk into a thick, but runny batter. On a shallow plate, combine the panko breadcrumbs, remaining ¼ teaspoon cayenne pepper and paprika.

Place the seitan in the batter, evenly coat it and allow for any excess to drip off. Transfer it into the panko mixture and evenly coat it. Transfer the roast to the baking sheet and roast it in the oven for 25 to 30 minutes, until golden.

Slice the crunchy roast to serve. It is best served immediately and great alongside roast potatoes, mushroom scallops, garlic and herb dip and roasted red pepper gravy! You can also enjoy the roast the next day. To get it crispy again, reheat it in the oven.

BEETROOT SEITAN ROAST

This beetroot seitan roast packs a good bite, and it's a guaranteed winner at the dinner table! I love pan-roasting my seitan roasts to give them a slightly crispy and flavorful layer, so I've included this delicious technique with this recipe. It's great for a roast dinner and it makes for a delicious leftover sandwich—just sayin'!

Serves 4 to 6

For the Seitan

½ cup (50 g) chickpea flour (gram flour)

1½ cups (200 g) vital wheat gluten

1 tbsp (7 g) onion powder

1 tsp garlic powder

2 tsp (4 g) dried oregano

2 tsp (2 g) dried rosemary

1 tsp Chinese five-spice mix

3 tbsp (15 g) nutritional yeast

2 tbsp (32 g) tomato paste

5.3 oz (150 g) fresh peeled and finely shredded beetroot

2 cups (473 ml) vegetable stock

3 tbsp (43 g) softened vegan butter

1 tsp marmite/vegemite

1 tbsp (15 ml) maple syrup

1 tbsp (15 ml) tamari

For Frying

2–3 tbsp (30–45 ml) olive oil, divided

2 finely sliced red onions

1 tbsp (14 g) light brown sugar, packed

2–3 fresh sage leaves (optional)

Combine the chickpea flour, vital wheat gluten, onion powder, garlic powder, oregano, rosemary, five-spice mix and nutritional yeast in a large mixing bowl with a spatula. In a large bowl, whisk together the tomato paste, shredded beetroot, vegetable stock, vegan butter, marmite/vegemite, maple syrup and tamari.

Slowly pour half of the wet mixture into the dry mixture while stirring with a wooden spoon. Place the other half of the liquid ingredients in the fridge.

Once the dough becomes too sticky to handle with the spoon, switch to using your hands. Combine all the ingredients thoroughly, then transfer the dough to a lightly floured surface and knead for 5 minutes to develop the gluten. Place the dough back into your mixing bowl, cover and place it in the fridge for 30 minutes.

After 20 minutes, preheat your oven to 390°F (200°C). Place a rack in the middle of the oven and place an ovenproof container filled with about 70 ounces (2 L) of water into the bottom of your oven.

After 30 minutes, give the dough another quick knead, then shape it into a log and tightly wrap it in about three to four layers of strong aluminum foil. Bake it for 30 minutes. Once the time elapses, allow the roast to cool in the oven with the oven door shut. It should take about 1½ to 2 hours to cool completely before removing it from the oven.

To get a nice crust, heat 2 tablespoons (30 ml) of olive oil in a cast-iron or nonstick pan over medium-high heat. Place the sliced red onions in the pan and allow them to cook for a few minutes until softened. Then add the brown sugar and cook for 8 to 10 minutes, until the onions begin to caramelize and brown.

(continued)

For Serving

Creamy Cauliflower Bake with Caramelized Onions (page 112)

Pecan and Apple Stuffing (page 107)

Red Wine Gravy (page 136)

Unwrap the roast and place it in your pan. Carefully turn it every minute for 10 minutes to give it a nice crust all around. Remove the rest of your liquid ingredients from the fridge and carefully pour half of it into the pan with the roast. Continue to turn the roast. When most of the liquid has evaporated, pour in the rest. Pan-glaze the roast for a total of 10 to 15 minutes, or until a nice and flavorful crust has built on the outside of your roast. Then remove it from the pan.

To decorate the roast, crispy fry a couple of fresh sage leaves in 1 tablespoon (15 ml) of oil over medium heat and sprinkle them over the roast, if desired.

To serve, slice the roast into discs about 1 to 2 inches (2.5 to 5 cm) thick. Serve the caramelized onions alongside, or utilize them in a side dish such as a cauliflower bake, some delicious stuffing or a flavorful gravy.

CREAMY MUSHROOM AND LAGER ROAST

When it comes to mushrooms, there's only one thing I can tell you: the more, the merrier! As the mushroom lover that I am, it comes with no surprise that you can find not one but two servings of mushrooms in this creamy seitan roast! This seitan is created with a two-layer marbling, one of which includes blended mushrooms and a seasoning mix full of flavor. To create the delicious texture and keep the roast wonderfully succulent, it is fried in hoppy lager, which perfectly complements the earthy flavors of the mushrooms and takes this roast to a whole new level. To prepare this delicious roast ahead of time, place the roast in the fridge for up to three days after braising, then panfry and create the creamy mushroom sauce on the day of serving.

Serves 4

For the Seitan

2 tbsp (30 ml) olive oil

17.6 oz (500 g) roughly chopped chestnut or portobello mushrooms

3 tbsp (10 g) rubbed sage

1 tbsp (3 g) fresh thyme

3 tsp (15 g) minced garlic

¼ cup (60 ml) lager

1 tbsp (5 g) instant coffee granules

2 tsp (8 g) smoked salt

2 tsp (5 g) onion powder

1 tsp ground coriander

1 tsp smoked paprika

1 tsp ginger powder

½ tsp white pepper

¼ tsp ground cloves

1 cup (240 ml) water

3 cups (420 g) vital wheat gluten

Heat 2 tablespoons (30 ml) of olive oil in a large, nonstick skillet over medium-high heat. Add the roughly chopped mushrooms and cook for 5 minutes, stirring frequently. Add the rubbed sage, thyme and garlic to the skillet. Cook for 5 to 10 minutes, or until the mushrooms have released most of their water and the majority has evaporated. Deglaze the skillet with the lager and remove it from the heat.

Carefully transfer the mushrooms to a food processor with the instant coffee, smoked salt, onion powder, coriander, smoked paprika, ground ginger, white pepper and ground cloves. Pulse for 20 to 30 seconds, or until the mushrooms are mostly broken down. Slowly add the water to the processor and process until smooth.

Switch to a dough hook in the food processor, or transfer the mixture to a large mixing bowl and use a wooden spoon or spatula. Slowly add the vital wheat gluten and continue to combine until you get a firm dough ball. Switch to using your hands and knead the dough ball on a lightly floured surface for 3 minutes until smooth.

Place the dough ball back in a bowl and set it aside to rest.

(continued)

For the 'Fat' Layer

1 cup (140 g) vital wheat gluten

1 tsp onion powder

½ tsp white pepper

¼ cup (60 ml) olive oil

⅓ cup (80 ml) soymilk

For Panfrying

2½ tbsp (37 ml) olive oil, divided

1 cup (240 ml) lager

2 tbsp (30 ml) tamari

For the Creamy Mushroom Sauce

½ tbsp (7 ml) olive oil

2 cups (200 g) roughly sliced brown mushrooms

Pinch of sea salt

½ cup (50 g) sliced shallots

¼ cup (60 ml) lager

¼ tsp ground black pepper

1 cup (240 ml) vegetable stock

½ cup (125 ml) dairy-free cream

1 tbsp (15 ml) tamari

For Serving

The Perfect Roast Potatoes (page 104)

Vegan Yorkies (page 108)

In the meantime, let's prepare the "fat" part for our seitan! In a fresh mixing bowl, combine the vital wheat gluten, onion powder and white pepper. Pour in the olive oil and soymilk, and knead into a loose dough ball.

Divide the first (mushroom) dough ball into four parts, and the second ("fat layer") dough ball into three parts. On a nonstick surface, roll each piece of the dough into a rectangle of about ½ inch (1 cm) thick. Try to make each dough piece roughly the same shape, but don't worry about being too neat with it. Then layer the pieces on top of each other, with one "fat" layer between each mushroom layer. This will create the lovely marbling in this seitan roast!

To panfry: Heat 2 tablespoons (30 ml) of olive oil in a large, nonstick skillet over medium-high heat. Fry the seitan for 2 minutes, then carefully flip and fry for 2 minutes on the second side. Pour the lager in the skillet and reduce the heat. Cover the skillet with a lid and simmer over low heat for 10 minutes. Flip the seitan and fry for 10 to 15 minutes without the lid, until the majority of the lager has evaporated and the seitan edges have slightly caramelized. Remove the seitan from the skillet and place it in the fridge to rest for at least 1 hour or for up to 3 days.

To create the creamy mushroom sauce: Heat ½ tablespoon (7 ml) of the olive oil in the skillet over medium heat. Add the mushrooms and salt. Cook for 2 to 3 minutes, then add the shallots. Cook for 10 to 15 minutes, or until the mushrooms have released most of their moisture and the shallots have slightly caramelized. Deglaze the skillet with the lager, then stir in the black pepper and vegetable stock. Simmer for 8 to 10 minutes. Stir in the dairy-free cream and tamari. Place the seitan in the sauce. Close the skillet with a lid and simmer for 5 minutes, then you're ready to serve!

To finish panfrying: Carefully cut the seitan into ½- to 1-inch (1- to 2.5-cm) slices. Heat the remaining ½ tablespoon (7 ml) of the olive oil in a large nonstick pan. Fry the slices on each side for 2 to 3 minutes, or until golden. Deglaze the pan with the 2 tablespoons (30 ml) of tamari and remove the slices from the heat. Serve with the creamy mushroom sauce, roast potatoes and Yorkies!

STANDOUT SIDEKICKS

Every hero has a sidekick who is important to making the team come together: Batman and Robin, Elsa and Olaf and C-3PO and R2-D2. And on the dinner table, one thing is for sure: All the heroines and heroes wouldn't shine their brightest light without their treasured sidekicks! In this chapter, we will discover the companions that truly make our showstoppers stand out. They lift up the main characters on the table and promote them to the superheroes that they are.

There is something mouthwatering for everyone in this chapter: A traditional British-style Sunday roast needs potatoes, like the Perfect Roast Potatoes on page 104; Yorkies, like my vegan version on page 108; and stuffing, like my pecan and apple variety on page 107. Or maybe you love to get outside of your roast-comfort-zone with a Savory Sweet Potato–Peanut Crumble (page 120), Chilli Cheeze Corn Bread Dumplings (page 116) and Parsnip and Miso Mash (page 124). I assure you, you will find something in this part of the book that will blow your mind and have everyone at the dinner table totally impressed.

THE PERFECT ROAST POTATOES

A classic! Roast potatoes are a must for a traditional roast meal. They are crunchy on the outside, soft on the inside and they simply hit the spot. Traditionally, roast potatoes are cooked in goose fat for the perfect texture. In this recipe adaptation, I'm showing you how to achieve the perfect outer crisp and fluffy inside with simple vegan ingredients. Time to tuck in!

Serves 4 to 6

For the Potatoes

28 oz (800 g) peeled potatoes, cut into bite-size chunks

1 tbsp (10 g) baking soda

2 tbsp (28 g) vegan butter

3 tsp (15 g) crushed garlic

1 tbsp (2 g) fresh thyme

1 tbsp (2 g) fresh rosemary

2 tsp (2 g) fresh sage leaves

¾ tsp sweet paprika

½ tsp sea salt

For Serving

Any of the roasts in this book!

Place the peeled and cubed potatoes in a large bowl. Add enough water to submerge the potatoes. Add the baking soda, then give it a stir to combine. Let the potatoes rest in the water for at least 30 minutes, then discard the water.

Transfer the potatoes to a large saucepan, cover them in fresh water and bring to a boil. Once boiling, cook for 5 minutes before draining the water. Place a lid on top of the saucepan and give the potatoes a good shake to "fluff up" their edges. Transfer them to an ovenproof dish.

Preheat your oven to 390°F (200°C).

Melt the vegan butter in a small saucepan. Add the garlic, thyme, rosemary and sage. Fry for 3 to 4 minutes, until fragrant. Remove from the heat and stir in the sweet paprika.

Drizzle the melted butter through a fine-mesh sieve right over the potatoes. Set the strained herbs aside. Sprinkle the potatoes with the sea salt. Roast for 35 to 45 minutes, until the potatoes are crispy, tossing them halfway through.

Remove the potatoes from the oven and add the herbs back into the mixture, and give it a good mix. Serve with your favorite roast and gravy on the side. Roast potatoes are super versatile and a must-have ingredient to a traditional roast dinner, so pair them up with any of the roasts and sauces in this book.

PECAN AND APPLE STUFFING

I can't believe it's taken me to adult age to first try homemade stuffing. It wasn't much of a thing where I grew up in Germany. And I can tell you I've been obsessed since I first made it! It's a great roast filling and a great side, filled with wonderful umami and comfort flavors. This Pecan and Apple Stuffing brings a load of tangy and sweet aromas with a delicious crunchiness from the pecans. It's super festive and mouthwatering all year round!

Swap out the bread for gluten-free bread in this recipe. It's just as delicious! This stuffing goes well as a side with pretty much every recipe in this book, and it's a fantastic addition to your roast dinner!

Serves 4 to 6

For the Stuffing

1 tbsp (15 ml) canola oil

1 cup (160 g) chopped onion

1 large apple, cut into ½-inch (1-cm) cubes

2 tbsp (30 ml) balsamic vinegar

1¾ cups (200 g) peeled and finely diced carrots

1¼ cups (150 g) finely diced celery

2 cups (200 g) bread, ripped into bite-size chunks

½ cup (50 g) chopped pecans plus ¼ cup (25 g) whole pecans

2 tbsp (16 g) sunflower or pumpkin seeds (optional)

4 sprigs rosemary

2 tbsp (6 g) fresh sage leaves

2 cups (473 ml) vegetable stock

Preheat your oven to 390°F (200°C).

Heat the canola oil in a large saucepan over medium heat. Add the onion and fry for 3 to 5 minutes, until translucent. Add the apple and cook for 5 minutes, until the apple begins to soften and caramelize. Add the balsamic vinegar to deglaze the pan. Add the carrots and celery. Cook for 2 minutes, then remove everything from the heat.

Place your bread chunks in a large mixing bowl. Add the pecans, sunflower seeds (if using), rosemary and sage. Give them a good stir and add your apple mixture. Combine everything, then transfer the mixture to an 8 x 6–inch (20 x 15–cm) ovenproof dish.

Pour the vegetable stock over the dish and bake for 30 minutes. Serve it hot alongside the rest of your roast dinner.

VEGAN YORKIES

Traditionally, Yorkshire puds are made in a specific tray and, as they are originally made from mostly egg, they rise wonderfully in those. For the perfect vegan Yorkshire pudding, I love making these in a large muffin pan. It is much better at giving you the well-known shape for your puds. To make these delicious Yorkies rise to the occasion—pun intended—it's important that the oil in the muffin pan is piping hot before you add the batter, so please handle the tray with the utmost care!

Serves 6

For the Yorkshire Pudding

6 tbsp (84 ml) vegetable oil

¾ cup (100 g) all-purpose flour

1 cup (130 g) cornstarch

2 tsp (9 g) baking powder

1 tsp baking soda

1¼ cups (300 ml) plant milk

1 tbsp (15 ml) apple cider vinegar

For Serving

The Perfect Roast Potatoes (page 104)

Your favorite gravy

Preheat your oven to 450°F (232°C).

Pour 1 tablespoon (15 ml) of vegetable oil into each muffin hole of a six-hole muffin pan. Place it in the preheated oven and heat the oil for 20 minutes, until steaming hot.

In the meantime, combine the all-purpose flour, cornstarch, baking powder and baking soda in a medium-sized mixing bowl. In a separate bowl, mix the plant milk and apple cider vinegar. Set it aside for 10 minutes to curdle.

When the oil is steaming hot, pour the wet into the dry mixture and quickly whisk to combine. Carefully remove the hot muffin pan from the oven and quickly pour the batter into the hot oil, about ¾ cup (185 ml).

Quickly move the muffin pan back to the oven for 10 to 13 minutes, until risen and golden.

Remove the Yorkies from the muffin pan and carefully move them to a kitchen towel to remove any excess oil. Serve immediately alongside your roast potatoes and cover in gravy—simply the best!

MAPLE-ROASTED SWEET POTATOES

If I had to describe these Maple-Roasted Sweet Potatoes in two words, they would be: utterly addictive. After eating an entire serving in one sitting, I'm the best proof! Salt and maple have forever been a dream team in my book. Combined with cubed sweet potato and toasted pecans, this recipe is the master of sweet and salty flavor combinations! And did you know that pecans taste like nutty candy, once toasted?

Serves 4 to 6

For the Sweet Potatoes

9 cups (990 g) cubed, peeled sweet potatoes

3 tbsp (45 ml) olive oil, divided

3.5 oz (100 g) smoked tofu, cut into small cubes

1 tbsp (15 ml) tamari

1 cup (110 g) pecan halves

¼ cup (60 ml) maple syrup

2 tsp (12 g) sea salt flakes

For Serving

Mini Apple and Sage Roasties (page 29) or BBQ-Roasted Pineapple (page 41)

Preheat your oven to 320°F (160°C). Line a baking sheet with parchment paper.

Place the sweet potatoes and 1 tablespoon (15 ml) of olive oil in a large bowl. Toss to coat evenly, then spread them out on a baking sheet in a single layer. Roast for 20 to 25 minutes, or until soft.

In the meantime, heat the remainder of the olive oil over medium-high heat in a large, nonstick skillet. Add the tofu cubes and crispy fry them for 5 to 10 minutes, tossing frequently, until all sides are evenly golden and lightly crispy. Reduce the heat to low and deglaze the pan with the tamari. Stir to evenly coat the tofu and cook for 1 to 2 minutes, until the liquid has evaporated and the tofu is coated. Remove the pan from the heat.

Place the pecans on the baking sheet and toast them in the oven for 8 to 10 minutes. Check on them once a minute to ensure they don't burn, and give them a toss halfway through.

Once done, combine the roasted sweet potato, tofu cubes and pecans in a serving dish. Drizzle with maple syrup and coat everything, then sprinkle salt flakes over the top. Serve right away.

This flavor-explosion of a recipe is best served alongside mini apple and sage roasties or BBQ-roasted pineapple for the ultimate sweet-savory combo!

CREAMY CAULIFLOWER BAKE WITH CARAMELIZED ONIONS

Forget cauliflower cheese—this creamy cauliflower bake is where it's at! The buttery sauce is full of nutritional yeast, miso paste and lemon juice to give it a hearty flavor. Cashews, potato, carrot and oats create a wonderfully thick and creamy texture. It's heavenly, especially topped with caramelized onions and some almond flakes for a perfect crunch! If you're gluten-free, make sure to use gluten-free oats in this recipe.

Serves 4 to 6 (side) or 2 to 3 (main)

For the Cauliflower Bake

¼ cup (30 g) cashews

1 head cauliflower, cut into florets

⅓ cup (40 g) roughly chopped white potato

½ cup (60 g) roughly chopped carrot

1 tbsp (8 g) white miso paste

2 cups (473 ml) plant milk

2 tbsp (12 g) rolled oats

½ tsp sea salt

¼ tsp ground black pepper

¼ tsp sweet paprika

3 tbsp (15 g) nutritional yeast

1 tbsp (15 ml) fresh lemon juice

2 tbsp (30 ml) melted virgin coconut oil

2 tbsp (30 ml) olive oil

2 finely sliced red onions

1 tbsp (14 g) light brown sugar, packed

¼ cup (27 g) almond flakes

For Serving

The Perfect Roast Potatoes (page 104)

Your favorite roast

Place your cashews in a small heatproof bowl and cover them with boiling water. Set them aside to soak for 20 minutes, then drain.

In the meantime, steam your cauliflower, potato and carrot separately over a saucepan filled with steaming water, until softened. Set the cauliflower florets aside.

Place the potato and carrot in a blender or food processor. Add the white miso paste, plant milk, oats, salt, black pepper, paprika, nutritional yeast, lemon juice, coconut oil and the drained cashews. Blend on high for 3 to 4 minutes, until you get a smooth sauce.

Combine the cauliflower and sauce in a bowl. Transfer the mixture to a greased, ovenproof dish, then preheat your oven to 390°F (200°C).

Heat the olive oil in a large, nonstick skillet over medium heat. Fry the red onions for 3 to 5 minutes, until translucent. Add the brown sugar and cook for 8 to 10 minutes, stirring frequently, until the onions caramelize.

Top the cauliflower bake with the caramelized onions and almond flakes. Place the ovenproof dish into the oven and bake for 8 to 10 minutes, or until the top turns golden. Serve hot alongside roast potatoes and your favorite roast.

RANCH POTATO MASH

Potatoes and ranch seasoning are a flavor marriage made in heaven! This simple, well-seasoned potato mash is great to switch up things and replace the roast potatoes in a filling roast meal—but you can go double-tater and have roast potatoes with it too! To create the wonderful buttery texture, we're adding vegan mayonnaise to the mash alongside white wine vinegar for the perfect acidity and creaminess.

Serves 4 to 6

For the Mash

32 oz (900 g) white potatoes, peeled and roughly diced

2 tbsp (30 ml) vegan mayonnaise

¼ cup (60 ml) plant milk

1–3 tsp (5–15 ml) white wine vinegar

1 tbsp (2 g) dried parsley, plus fresh parsley, for garnish (optional)

1 tsp dried dill

1 tsp onion powder

½ tsp garlic powder

½ tsp sea salt

¼ tsp ground black pepper

For Serving

Sticky Tempeh Parcels (page 54)

Roasted Red Pepper Gravy (page 144)

Peel your potatoes and cube them into bite-size pieces. Place the potatoes in a large saucepan, cover them with salted water and boil over high heat for 20 to 25 minutes until cooked. Drain the water and place the potatoes back in the empty saucepan.

Mash the potatoes in the saucepan, then add the vegan mayonnaise, plant milk and white wine vinegar. Stir until well combined.

Add the dried parsley, dried dill, onion powder, garlic powder, salt and black pepper. Stir through all the seasonings to evenly distribute them throughout your potato mash. Garnish with fresh parsley, if using, then serve hot with sticky tempeh parcels and roasted red pepper gravy.

CHILLI CHEEZE CORN BREAD DUMPLINGS

Corn bread is a well-loved must-have for any Thanksgiving dinner. But you haven't seen corn bread's full potential until you've tried these chilli cheeze stuffed corn bread dumplings! Crunchy on the outside with a simple cornmeal coating, these dumplings are filled with spicy jalapeños for a little kick and vegan cheese that melts gloriously. This is best served straight from the oven.

Serves 3 to 4

For the Dumplings

3 cups (710 ml) vegetable stock

1 cup (145 g) fine cornmeal

½ cup (70 g) flour

1 tbsp (14 g) golden caster sugar

2 tbsp (12 g) nutritional yeast

¼ tsp sea salt

¼ cup (60 ml) pickled jalapeño juice

2 tbsp (30 ml) sunflower oil

¼ cup (60 ml) plant milk

2 tbsp (27 g) finely chopped pickled jalapeños

8–10 (½-inch [1-cm]) cubes vegan cheddar-style cheese

½ cup (90 g) coarse cornmeal

For Serving

Tangy Harissa Carrot Dip (page 155)

Miso Onion Gravy (page 139)

Heat the vegetable stock in a large saucepan over medium-high heat.

In the meantime, combine the fine cornmeal, flour, golden caster sugar, nutritional yeast and salt in a large mixing bowl. In a separate bowl, combine the pickled jalapeño juice, sunflower oil, milk and pickled jalapeños.

Create a well in the middle of the dry ingredients and pour the jalapeño mixture in. Stir to combine until you get a firm dough. Set it aside for 10 minutes.

Use a tablespoon to portion the corn bread mixture into eight to ten dumplings. Press a vegan cheese cube into the middle of each dumpling, then roll the dumpling between your palms to create an evenly round shape.

Carefully transfer the dumplings into the simmering broth over medium-low heat and allow them to simmer for 30 minutes, stirring frequently to prevent them from getting stuck to the bottom of your pan. In the meantime, preheat your oven to 350°F (177°C) and place a rack in the middle. Line a baking sheet with parchment paper.

Drain and roll the dumplings in the coarse cornmeal, and transfer them to the baking sheet. Bake for 15 to 20 minutes, or until crispy and golden.

Serve hot and as a starter alongside harissa carrot dip or as a side with miso onion gravy—simply delicious!

GARLIC BUTTER MUSHROOM SCALLOPS

Mushrooms are a must for me when it comes to a satisfying roast meal, and I've never quite been able to understand people that don't like mushrooms at all. Panfrying mushrooms brings out their mouthwatering natural umami and with their smooth texture and wonderful bite, they're basically the perfect addition to a flavorful roast meal. For this recipe, I'm using king oyster mushrooms. With their thick stems they're ideal for slicing and scoring, and they wonderfully soak up the aromas of the garlic and thyme.

Serves 2 to 4

For the Scallops

14 oz (400 g) king oyster mushrooms

4 tbsp (56 g) vegan butter

4 tsp (20 g) crushed garlic

Pinch of sea salt

2 tsp (4 g) fresh thyme

For Serving

Parsnip and Miso Mash (page 124)

Teriyaki Seitan Steak (page 91)

Slice the king oyster mushrooms into ½- to 1-inch (1- to 2.5-cm) pieces. Use a small sharp knife to cut a crisscross pattern into the surfaces of the slices, about 0.04 to 0.08 inch (1 to 2 mm) deep.

Melt the vegan butter in a large, nonstick pan over medium heat. Add the garlic and a pinch of salt. Set the mushroom slices into the pan flat and fry for 3 for 4 minutes, until the bottoms become golden. Flip and repeat on the second side.

When the second side is just about done, sprinkle in your fresh thyme, and cook for 1 minute. Remove from the heat and serve immediately. Spoon the melted garlic butter and thyme over the mushroom scallops when serving.

Serve alongside parsnip mash and a delicious teriyaki seitan steak.

SAVORY SWEET POTATO-PEANUT CRUMBLE

A savory sweet potato crumble? YES! Don't judge it until you've tried it, I always like to say. This savory crumble is marvelous! I love combining sweet and savory flavors: The natural sweetness of the sweet potato pairs wonderfully with the nutty notes of peanut butter combined with tamari and lemon juice. You could almost call it a satay crumble, and doesn't that sound divine? You can easily make this dish ahead of time and store it in the fridge for up to three days, then reheat it on the day of serving.

Serves 6

For the Filling

2 lb (910 g) cubed, peeled and cooked sweet potato

2 tbsp (32 g) smooth peanut butter

1 tbsp (15 ml) fresh lemon juice

1 tbsp (15 ml) tamari

¼ tsp toasted sesame oil

1 tsp sriracha or hot sauce (optional)

1–2 tbsp (15–30 ml) water

1 cup (240 g) cooked and drained black beans

For the Crumble

¾ cup (120 g) all-purpose flour

¼ cup (20 g) nutritional yeast

½ tsp baking powder

½ tsp sea salt

¼ tsp onion powder

¼ tsp ground black pepper

¼ cup (57 g) butter

For Serving

Jackfruit Filo Mini Wellingtons (page 53)

Your favorite gravy

In a large bowl, mash the cooked sweet potato with a potato masher or the back of a fork. In a separate bowl, whisk together the peanut butter, lemon juice, tamari, sesame oil, sriracha (if using) and water until you get a smooth sauce.

Pour the sauce into the mashed sweet potato. Stir to combine, then mix in the cooked and drained black beans. Transfer the mixture to an ovenproof dish, evening out the top.

Preheat your oven to 400°F (204°C).

In the meantime, prepare your crumble topping: In a bowl, combine the flour, nutritional yeast, baking powder, salt, onion powder and pepper. Add the butter in small chunks, then massage them into the dry mixture with your hands until the mixture is crumbled. Sprinkle the crumbs over the mixture.

Bake the crumble for 25 to 35 minutes, or until the top is golden. This sweet potato and peanut crumble is delicious served with mini Wellingtons and your favorite gravy. This tastes scrumptious reheated too, and it's a great dish to make ahead of time. Simply keep it in the fridge for up to 3 days and reheat it on the day of serving.

ROASTED SPROUTS WITH SMOKY TOFU BITS

If you're not a fan of sprouts, forget everything you've learned about sprouts before and hear me out: These are not your average sprouts; these are cool sprouts. Got it? Okay, now let me show you how to actually make them taste great! Crispy fried and roasted. These sprouts are a game-changer. The addition of nutritional yeast and onion powder give them a divine cheese-and-onion vibe that everyone around the table will love! They're served with smoky tofu bites for a little extra umami and toasted almond flakes for a crunch.

Serves 4

For the Sprouts

1 tbsp (14 g) vegan butter

7 oz (200 g) Brussels sprouts

1 tbsp (5 g) nutritional yeast

1 tsp onion powder

½ tsp sea salt

¼ tsp ground black pepper

1 tbsp (15 ml) olive oil

1 tbsp (7 g) almond flakes

For the Smoky Tofu Bits

1 tbsp (15 ml) olive oil

3.5 oz (100 g) smoked tofu, cut into small cubes

1 tbsp (15 ml) tamari

For Serving

Roasted Eggplant Steak (page 25)

Roasted Red Pepper Gravy (page 144)

Preheat your oven to 375°F (190°C).

Melt the vegan butter in a large cast-iron or nonstick skillet over medium-high heat. Cut the Brussels sprouts in half and place them face down into the hot, melted butter. Fry for 12 to 15 minutes, until the bottoms of the sprouts begin to crisp, then remove them from the heat.

In a small bowl, combine the nutritional yeast, onion powder, salt, pepper and olive oil and brush onto the crispy side of the sprouts. Place them into an ovenproof dish in a single layer and roast them in the oven for 8 to 10 minutes, or until golden.

In the meantime, heat the olive oil in a medium, nonstick pan. Fry the tofu cubes in the hot oil for 4 to 5 minutes, tossing them frequently to crispy fry on all sides. Once crispy, drizzle in the tamari and stir until the liquid has evaporated, then remove from the heat.

Toast the almond flakes in the hot pan for 2 to 3 minutes, until golden. Serve the roasted Brussels sprouts mixed with the tofu cubes and topped with the toasted almonds. Take your roast meal to the next level by serving these alongside roasted eggplant steak and roasted red pepper gravy!

PARSNIP AND MISO MASH

With its distinctly salty and tangy taste, miso paste brings a delicious umami to this parsnip mash. For this recipe, I like to use white miso paste, which is lighter and sweeter than dark miso. It adds a wonderful cheesiness to the smooth parsnip mash. This is perfect alongside a scrumptious mushroom pie or steak, but also pairs well with crunchy textures such as the panko seitan roast or filo Wellingtons smothered in delicious brandy peppercorn sauce.

Serves 4

For the Mash

35 oz (992 g) peeled fresh parsnips

1 tbsp (14 g) vegan butter

7 oz (200 ml) plant milk (I like to use soymilk)

2½ tbsp (43 g) white miso paste

¼ tsp ground black pepper

Sea salt, to taste

Fresh herbs, such as dill or chives (optional)

Olive oil, for serving

For Serving

Any mushroom pie or steak

Crispy Chick'n-Style Panko Roast (page 93) or Jackfruit Filo Mini Wellingtons (page 53)

Cut the parsnips into bite-size pieces; there is no need to be too precise as the parsnips will be mashed later on. Add them to a medium-sized saucepan with lightly salted water and bring them to a boil. Simmer for 20 to 25 minutes over low-medium heat, or until the parsnip pieces are soft. Drain and add the parsnips to a medium-sized bowl.

Mash the parsnips with a potato masher or with the back of a fork, then add the vegan butter, plant milk, white miso paste and black pepper. Stir thoroughly to combine.

Season to taste with salt and serve topped with fresh herbs (if using) and a drizzle of olive oil. This parsnip and miso mash is delicious as an alternative to potatoes for your roast dinner and keeps things interesting for the feast. Its flavors are divine alongside mushroom-based mains, but also mouthwatering served alongside crunchy textures such as the panko roast or the mini Wellingtons.

SHREDDED BBQ CABBAGE

One thing I love about making roasts is that ingredients that might otherwise come across as boring or bland truly get a time to shine—such as this Shredded BBQ Cabbage! With a smoky sweet tomato sauce that complements the sharp roasted red cabbage perfectly, this recipe is super quick to make in a single skillet. It's delicious alongside BBQ pineapple and jackfruit Wellingtons.

Serves 4

For the Cabbage

1 head red cabbage (roughly 31 oz [879 g])

2 tbsp (30 ml) canola oil

½ tsp sea salt

1 tsp whole cumin seeds

2 tbsp (32 g) tomato paste

2 tbsp (30 ml) tamari

½ tsp smoked paprika

1 tbsp plus 1 tsp (20 ml) molasses

1 tbsp (15 ml) red wine vinegar

½ tsp chili flakes

½ tsp garlic powder

½ cup (125 ml) plus 2 tbsp (30 ml) water, divided

1 tsp cornstarch

For Serving

The Perfect Roast Potatoes (page 104)

BBQ Roasted Pineapple (page 41)

Jackfruit Filo Mini Wellingtons (page 53)

Brandy Peppercorn Sauce (page 140)

Shred your cabbage into thin strips using a mandolin or sharp knife.

Heat the canola oil in a large, nonstick skillet over medium-high heat. Add the shredded cabbage and cook, stirring frequently, for 5 minutes, or until the cabbage softens. Sprinkle in the salt and cumin seeds and continue to fry the cabbage for 10 to 15 minutes, stirring frequently, until cooked all the way through.

In the meantime, prepare your sauce: Whisk to combine the tomato paste, tamari, smoked paprika, molasses, red wine vinegar, chili flakes, garlic powder and ½ cup (125 ml) water in a bowl. In a small container, combine the cornstarch and 2 tablespoons (30 ml) of water into a smooth slurry. Stir it into the bowl and pour the mixture over the shredded cabbage.

Stir to evenly coat the cabbage in the sauce. Remove the skillet from the heat once the sauce is evenly distributed and begins to thicken. Serve immediately or store in the fridge overnight to reheat the next day! This is delicious alongside roast potatoes, BBQ pineapple and jackfruit filo mini wellingtons, with a drizzle of brandy peppercorn sauce!

CRUNCHY RUTABAGA FINGERS

Turning a roast dinner into a feast of different flavors and textures is the ultimate goal when creating a well-rounded, flavorful roast meal. Sides are a great way to introduce additional levels to the table. These rutabaga (swede) fingers are crunchy on the outside and soft on the inside, which makes them perfect to dip into sauces and mop up any leftover gravy. They also happen to be gluten-free, and the almond meal coating creates a tasty nutty addition that's irresistible.

Serves 2 to 4

For the Rutabaga Fingers

1 rutabaga (roughly 26 oz [740 g])

2 tbsp (30 ml) canola oil

¼ cup (25 g) almond meal

½ tsp garlic powder

½ tsp ground nutmeg

½ tsp sea salt

For Serving

Shallot and Chestnut Crunch Roast (page 18)

Your favorite gravy

Tangy Harissa Carrot Dip (page 155)

Preheat your oven to 375°F (190°C). Line a baking sheet with parchment paper.

Peel the rutabaga, then cut it into ½-inch (1-cm) slices and then into fingers of about ½ inch (1 cm) thick. Place them in a bowl and toss them in the oil.

In a separate small bowl, combine the almond meal, garlic powder, nutmeg and salt. Add the mixture to the rutabaga and stir to generously coat the rutabaga fingers.

Transfer the rutabaga to the baking sheet and arrange the fingers so they don't touch. Bake for 25 to 30 minutes, or until crispy around the edges.

Serve alongside a delicious chestnut roast, your favorite gravy and the harissa carrot dip.

SMOKY CRUSTED GREEN BEANS

Delicious doesn't have to be complicated! While I love spending time in the kitchen and experimenting with different ingredients, I'm also a fan of simple and easy—especially when it comes to adding scrumptious sides to the dinner table. These crusted green beans are a perfect example! Tossed in aquafaba (chickpea water) and coated in a crunchy layer of polenta with a smoky seasoning, these green beans are so easy to throw together. They are super versatile and you can easily serve them as a side dish with any of the roasts in this book. They are delicious as a side and/or starter dunked in garlic and herb white bean dip! To make this gluten-free, swap out the polenta for the same amount of almond meal.

Serves 4

For the Green Beans

¼ cup (60 ml) aquafaba (chickpea water)

½ cup (90 g) coarse polenta

½ tsp onion powder

½ tsp smoked paprika

¼ tsp garlic powder

¼ tsp sea salt

¼ tsp ground black pepper

3 cups (477 g) trimmed green beans

For Serving

Roasted Garlic and Herb White Bean Dip (page 151)

Tangy Harissa Carrot Dip (page 155)

Preheat your oven to 375°F (190°C). Line a baking sheet with parchment paper.

Place your aquafaba in a mixing bowl and whip with an electric whisk for 10 to 12 minutes, or until stiff peaks form.

In a separate bowl, combine the coarse polenta, onion powder, smoked paprika, garlic powder, salt and black pepper.

Place your washed and dried beans into the aquafaba mix, giving everything a good mix to evenly coat the beans, then transfer the beans into the polenta mix. Toss to evenly coat the beans in the crumbs, then transfer the beans to the baking sheet in a single layer.

Bake for 20 to 25 minutes, or until golden and crispy. Serve these versatile crusted green beans as part of your main feast or as a starter. Add a delicious white bean dip or harissa carrot dip alongside. Scrumptious!

STUFFED TOMATOES

I first ate stuffed tomatoes at a restaurant on New Year's Eve almost twenty years ago and it's stuck in my head since. The juicy stuffed tomatoes were heavenly! For my own version of this very delicious memory, I filled large beef tomatoes with a yummy rice-and-spinach mixture, seasoned with nutritional yeast for some cheesiness and black pepper and chickpea flour to add a little bit of eggy-ness to the taste buds. Super simple, yet mouthwatering—try it for yourself!

Serves 6

For the Tomatoes

4 oz (113 g) frozen spinach

1 cup (190 g) white basmati rice

2 cups (473 ml) water

½ tsp plus a pinch of sea salt

1 tsp olive oil

⅓ cup (53 g) finely diced yellow onion

2 tsp (10 g) crushed garlic

1.1 oz (30 g) fresh flat-leaf parsley

6 large beefsteak tomatoes (roughly 4 lb [1.8 kg])

2 tbsp (10 g) nutritional yeast

½ tsp ground black pepper

½ cup (49 g) chickpea flour (gram flour)

¼ tsp black salt (kala namak) for some extra eggy flavor! (optional)

⅔ cup (158 ml) soymilk

1 tbsp (15 ml) fresh lemon juice

For Serving

Roasted Red Pepper Gravy (page 144)

Roasted Sesame Tempeh Fingers (page 61)

Leave the frozen spinach out to thaw for at least 30 minutes and preheat your oven to 380°F (193°C).

Wash the rice and discard the water. Place the rice in a saucepan with the water and a pinch of salt, cover with a lid and bring to a boil over medium-high heat. Once it boils, reduce the heat to low and leave the lid on the saucepan. Let the rice absorb the water for 10 to 15 minutes, until the rice is fluffy.

Heat the olive oil in a large, nonstick skillet. Add the onion and cook for 2 to 3 minutes, until translucent. Add the garlic and cook for 2 minutes, then add the thawed spinach. Stir to combine and cook for 3 to 4 minutes over low heat, until the majority of the liquid in the pan has evaporated.

In the meantime, chop the parsley in a food processor, then combine the parsley with the spinach and cooked rice in a bowl.

Cut off the top 1 inch (2.5 cm) of all the beef tomatoes and use a small spoon to scoop out the tomato flesh and seeds

Combine the nutritional yeast, the remaining salt, black pepper, chickpea flour, black salt (if using) and soymilk in a large bowl. Pour the mixture into the rice bowl. Drizzle in the fresh lemon juice. Stuff the hollow tomatoes with the mixture.

Place the tomatoes in an ovenproof dish and roast for 40 to 45 minutes.

Serve with roasted red pepper gravy and roasted sesame tempeh fingers.

SAUCES, DIPS AND CO.

What would a roast dinner be without all the luscious sauces? These are definitely my personal highlight on the table. Whether it's a glorious Sunday roast, a family get-together or a festive occasion, a comforting drizzle is a must. The limit does not exist and the more the merrier!

Most of the time, I create my gravies from scratch so they pack the most flavor! To make things easier, I often cook my gravies, sauces and dips in bulk by doubling, tripling and sometimes even quadrupling recipes. I keep any extras portion-sized and frozen in the freezer for when I need a quick and easy extra drizzle. If there are any bits left over after a roast meal, that is, of course!

Often you will find me drizzling a little extra onto my plate to soak it up with the last bit of pecan and apple stuffing or to fill that glorious Yorkie to the brim. Is your mouth watering yet? Good, then keep reading and find out how to make drool-worthy vegan Red Wine Gravy (page 136), flavorful Brandy Peppercorn Sauce (page 140), a luscious Roasted Garlic and Herb White Bean Dip (page 151) and more.

RED WINE GRAVY

What would a roast dinner be without a mouthwatering gravy? Exactly. It's one of those things where there can never be too much, and a roast dinner without a good gravy is simply not complete. This red wine gravy is my go-to when making a roast dinner—it's easy to make and so full of drool-worthy flavors with the rich caramelized onion and full-bodied red wine. It's the perfect sauce for roast potatoes, if you ask me!

Serves 4

For the Gravy

1 tbsp (15 ml) olive oil

1½ cups (150 g) finely sliced red onion

Pinch of sea salt

1 tsp light brown sugar, packed

2 tsp (10 g) crushed garlic

2 cups (473 ml) vegan red wine

1 cup (240 ml) vegetable stock

1 bay leaf

1 tsp cornstarch

2 tbsp (30 ml) water

For Serving

The Perfect Roast Potatoes (page 104)

Vegan Yorkies (page 108)

Orange-Glazed Seitan Ham (page 87)

Heat the olive oil in a medium-sized saucepan over medium heat. Add the onion, and sprinkle in the salt. Sauté for 2 to 3 minutes, or until it begins to soften, then stir in the brown sugar and cook for 1 minute. Add the garlic, then pour in the vegan red wine to deglaze the saucepan.

Stir in the vegetable stock and add the bay leaf. Bring to a boil and allow the sauce to simmer with a lid on for 10 to 15 minutes. Strain to remove the onion, garlic and bay leaf. Discard the bay leaf, but feel free to serve the onion and garlic mixture alongside your roast—it's full of flavor! Return the gravy to the stove.

In a small bowl, combine the cornstarch and water. Whisk it into the gravy. Continue to heat over low heat and stir until the gravy begins to thicken. Remove the gravy from the heat and serve hot with roast potatoes, Yorkies and glazed seitan ham.

MISO ONION GRAVY

Bring the full umami experience to the table with this scrumptuous miso gravy! While light in color, it packs a depth of flavor that's amazing with tofu and vegetable roasts. If you're gluten-free, swap the flour for one teaspoon of cornstarch.

Serves 4

For the Gravy

2 tbsp (28 g) vegan butter

¾ cup (240 g) finely chopped yellow onion

3 tsp (15 g) minced garlic

1 tsp tamari

1 tbsp (15 g) all-purpose flour

2¼ cups (532 ml) vegetable stock

2 tbsp (32 g) white miso paste

For Serving

The Perfect Roast Potatoes (page 104)

Your choice of steamed vegetables

Stuffed Tofu Roast with Spinach and Walnuts (page 58) or Stuffed Hasselback Squash (page 22)

Melt the vegan butter in a medium-sized saucepan over medium heat. Add the onion and sauté for 4 to 5 minutes, until translucent. Add the garlic and fry for 1 minute before deglazing the pan with the tamari.

Sprinkle in the all-purpose flour and give everything a good stir until it becomes a sticky paste. Slowly add half of the vegetable stock and stir well until the flour is well dissolved. Add the rest of the stock and bring to a simmer, then reduce the heat to low and simmer for 10 minutes with a lid on.

Stir in the white miso paste, then remove the saucepan from the heat and strain the gravy through a fine-mesh sieve.

Serve the sauce with roast potatoes, steamed vegetables and your favorite roast. It pairs well with the stuffed tofu roast and Hasselback squash.

BRANDY PEPPERCORN SAUCE

Looking for a great gravy that packs multiple levels of flavor? Then look no further because this Brandy Peppercorn Sauce will be right up your alley! Loaded with a comforting and rich peppery note, it warms up a meal on even the coldest of nights. This luscious sauce pairs well with a variety of roast dinners and is a great option if you're serving lots of different dishes on the dinner table. I love this sauce with anything mushroom flavored, such as the mushroom steak or the garlic and thyme mushroom pie.

Serves 3 to 4

For the Sauce

2 tbsp (28 g) vegan butter

2 shallots, finely sliced (roughly 3 oz [85 g])

½ tsp sea salt, plus more to taste

2 tsp (10 g) crushed garlic

1 tbsp (6 g) whole peppercorns

2 tbsp (30 ml) vegan brandy

1 tbsp (15 ml) tamari or coconut aminos

1 cup (240 ml) dairy-free cream

1 cup (240 ml) vegetable stock

1 tsp mushroom powder (optional)

Ground black pepper, to taste

1 tsp cornstarch

2 tbsp (30 ml) water

For Serving

Sticky Mushroom Steak (page 33) or Garlic and Thyme Mushroom Roast Pie (page 15)

Melt the vegan butter in a saucepan over medium heat. Add the shallots and sauté for 4 to 5 minutes, until translucent. Sprinkle in the salt after about 2 minutes.

Add the garlic and sauté for 1 minute. Sprinkle in the whole peppercorns and allow them to sit in the hot oil for 3 to 4 minutes before adding the brandy.

Let the brandy bubble away for a minute, then add the tamari. Simmer it all for 3 to 4 minutes, until you get a thick liquid in the saucepan.

Pour in the dairy-free cream and vegetable stock, then stir in the mushroom powder (if using). Add a lid to the saucepan and bring the sauce to a simmer. Cook for 10 minutes over low heat, stirring frequently, then season to taste with salt and black pepper.

Run the sauce through a fine-mesh sieve to remove the whole peppercorns and shallots. You can also leave them in the finished sauce. Make it the way you prefer! Mix the cornstarch with water to create a slurry, add it to the sauce and stir until the sauce thickens. Serve with your favorite roast. Why not try this one with the mushroom steak or the garlic and thyme mushroom roast pie?

LEMON MUSTARD SAUCE

Jazz up some roasted vegetables with this zesty lemon mustard sauce! This citrusy and creamy addition to the dinner table is the easiest way to spruce up a side of veg. Created with shallots and dill, it brings the fresh and light flavors of spring to the meal—but it's delightful any time of the year.

Serves 3 to 4

For the Sauce

1 tbsp (15 ml) olive oil

2–3 finely diced shallots (about 5 oz [150 g])

2 tbsp (30 ml) fresh lemon juice

1 tsp lemon zest

1 tbsp (15 ml) Dijon mustard

1 tbsp (15 ml) maple syrup

1 tsp chopped fresh dill, plus more for serving (optional)

1 cup (240 ml) dairy-free cream

1 cup (240 ml) vegetable stock

¼ tsp sea salt

Pinch of ground black pepper

1 tsp cornstarch

2 tbsp (30 ml) water

For Serving

Mushroom and Lentil Wellington (page 12) or Cranberry-Stuffed Turkey-Style Roast (page 67)

In a large, nonstick skillet, drizzle the olive oil over the shallots and gently fry them for 4 or 5 minutes, or until softened. Transfer the shallots to a food processor with the lemon juice, lemon zest, Dijon mustard and maple syrup. Process for 1 minute to combine the ingredients and break down the shallots further. Add the dill and pulse for 10 seconds to roughly combine it with the sauce.

Transfer the mixture to a large, nonstick saucepan over medium heat. Stir in the dairy-free cream, vegetable stock, salt and black pepper. Bring to a simmer and allow the sauce to cook for 5 minutes over low heat.

Combine the cornstarch with the water and whisk it into the sauce until the sauce begins to thicken, then remove it from the heat.

Drizzle the sauce on everything from boiled potatoes to asparagus and garnish with fresh dill, if you prefer. Serve the sauce with mushroom and lentil Wellington or cranberry-stuffed turkey-style roast.

ROASTED RED PEPPER GRAVY

Holy smokes! This gravy is just what you're looking for if—like me—you enjoy that sensation of sweet and smoky flavors! With oven-roasted sweet peppers as a base, this gravy packs a scrumptious zing. It's delightful alongside a number of vegan roasts, such as the crispy chick'n-style panko roast. It's also wonderful with roasted sprouts and cabbage steaks.

Serves 3 to 4

For the Gravy

2 red bell peppers (roughly 7.8 oz [220 g])

2 tbsp (30 ml) olive oil, divided

1 tbsp (14 g) light brown sugar, packed

1 tbsp (15 ml) tamari

1 tsp onion powder or granules

1 tsp garlic powder

1 tbsp (16 g) tomato paste

2 cups (473 ml) vegetable stock

1 tsp cornstarch

2 tbsp (30 ml) water

For Serving

Crispy Chick'n-Style Panko Roast (page 93)

Roasted Sprouts with Smoky Tofu Bits (page 123)

Preheat your oven to 390°F (200°C). Line a baking sheet with parchment paper.

Wash and remove the seeds from the red bell peppers, then roughly chop them and place them on the baking sheet. Drizzle with 1 tablespoon (15 ml) of olive oil and roast them in the oven for 25 to 30 minutes, until softened and lightly charred.

Combine the brown sugar with 1 tablespoon (15 ml) of olive oil in a medium-sized saucepan (with a lid). Place it uncovered over medium heat and dissolve the brown sugar.

Add the tamari, onion powder, garlic powder, tomato paste and vegetable stock to the saucepan. Add the roasted peppers and simmer for 20 minutes with the lid on.

Remove the sauce from the heat and transfer it to a blender. Blend on high until smooth, then return it to the saucepan over low heat.

In a small bowl, combine the cornstarch and water and stir it into the sauce. Continue to stir until the sauce thickens to your desired texture. Serve alongside crispy panko roast and roasted Brussels sprouts.

gluten-free

LEMON AND TARRAGON CASHEW CREAM

This tasty lemon and tarragon cream is inspired by French flavors including dried tarragon and fresh lemon juice. It's the perfect accompaniment for a well-rounded roast dinner. Delicious alongside roasted vegetables or as a spread for freshly toasted bread.

Serves 4 to 6

**For the Cashew Cream
(See Note)**

5.8 oz (165 g) cashews

2 tsp (10 g) white miso paste

1 tbsp (5 g) nutritional yeast

2 tbsp (30 ml) fresh lemon juice

1 tsp smoked salt

1 tbsp (3 g) dried tarragon

For Serving

Roasted vegetables or Smoky Crusted Green Beans (page 131)

Mushroom dish of your choice

Soak the cashews in water for 4 to 6 hours, or place them in boiling water for 20 minutes until softened.

Drain the cashews and transfer them to a high-speed food processor with the white miso paste, nutritional yeast, lemon juice and smoked salt. Process for 5 to 8 minutes, or until the cashew paste is smooth.

Sprinkle in the dried tarragon and process for 20 seconds to integrate the herbs.

Transfer the cashew cream to a small serving bowl, or keep it in an airtight container in the fridge for up to 5 days before serving.

Serve the cashew cream with roasted vegetables, such as asparagus or potatoes. It's also great with the green beans and any mushroom dishes.

Note: To make a pourable sauce, add ½ to ⅔ cup (120 to 158 ml) of vegetable stock to the food processor until the sauce has your desired texture, then heat it on the stove before serving.

SPICY RED PEPPER RELISH

Fruity and piquant, relish is usually a tasty addition to any cheeseboard. And believe me when I tell you it adds the perfect zing to your roast dinner! I love to include different tastes to fully satisfy all senses, and a tangy sauce obviously needs to be part of it. This well-seasoned red pepper relish has a delicious jalapeño spice, just enough for the sweet smoky taste of the roasted red peppers to come through. To serve, pair this relish with roasted vegetables for an extra kick. It's perfectly paired with BBQ-Roasted Pineapple (page 41), Roasted Eggplant Steak (page 25) and Shallot and Chestnut Roast (page 18).

Serves 3 to 4

For the Relish

14 oz (400 g) red bell peppers

5 oz (142 g) roughly chopped yellow onion

2 cloves garlic

7 oz (200 g) cherry tomatoes

1 tbsp (15 ml) olive oil

1 tbsp (10 g) pickled jalapeño

2 tbsp (30 ml) jalapeño pickle juice

1 tbsp (14 g) light brown sugar, packed

½ tsp sea salt

For Serving

Roasted veggies

Smoky Crusted Green Beans (page 131)

The Perfect Roast Potatoes (page 104)

Preheat your oven to 430°F (221°C). Line a baking sheet with parchment paper.

Place the whole red bell peppers onto the baking sheet. Roast them in the oven for roughly 20 minutes, or until the majority of the pepper skin is blackened.

Remove the tray from the oven and adjust the temperature to 390°F (200°C). Place the onion, garlic and cherry tomatoes in an ovenproof dish. Drizzle and toss in the olive oil, then transfer to the oven to roast for 15 minutes.

In the meantime, carefully peel off the skin from the bell peppers and remove the seeds. Transfer the roasted peppers to a food processor, then add the roasted onion, garlic and cherry tomatoes. Pulse the food processor for 20 seconds to break down the ingredients, then add the pickled jalapeño, pickle juice, brown sugar and salt. Pulse for 10 seconds.

Transfer the sauce to a small saucepan. Simmer on the lowest heat for 20 to 25 minutes, stirring frequently, until the mixture thickens.

Allow the relish to cool and then pour it into an airtight container. Place it in the fridge for up to 3 days until ready to enjoy. Serve the relish with roasted veggies, green beans or roast potatoes, or serve it as a dip.

ROASTED GARLIC AND HERB WHITE BEAN DIP

This cool and creamy dip uses white beans as a base, and it is delightful with roasted vegetables. The dip lifts up any simple roast dinner with a sweet tang from the caramelized, roasted garlic and fresh herbs, and it's a perfect addition to almost any meal. It's also great with toasted bread! If you don't have some of the herbs listed here, feel free to swap out any of these for what you have available.

Serves 3 to 4

For the Dip

2 whole bulbs garlic (roughly 55 g)

2 tbsp (30 ml) olive oil, divided

8.5 oz (240 g) canned cannellini or butter beans, drained

1 tbsp (4 g) fresh sage leaves

1 tbsp (2 g) fresh rosemary

1 tbsp (2 g) fresh thyme

1 tbsp (4 g) fresh parsley

Sea salt and ground black pepper, to taste

For Serving

The Perfect Roast Potatoes (page 104)

Stuffed Hasselback Squash (page 22)

Roasted veggies

Preheat your oven to 375°F (190°C).

Cut off the top ½ inch (1 cm) of the garlic bulbs. Place them on aluminum foil and drizzle with 1 tablespoon (15 ml) of olive oil. Cover the garlic with the foil and bake them for 20 to 25 minutes, or until soft and fragrant.

Add your beans to a food processor, then squeeze the soft, roasted garlic out of its peel and process until smooth and well combined. Add 1 tablespoon (15 ml) of olive oil into the mixture to help blend it smoothly.

Add the sage, rosemary, thyme and parsley. Blend in the processor for 30 seconds to break down and incorporate the herbs, then season to taste with salt and pepper.

Serve the dip with roast potatoes, Hasselback squash and roasted veggies.

CREAMY CHESTNUT HUMMUS WITH ROSEMARY

When it comes to sauces on the roast dinner table, my love of flavors and textures doesn't end with a drizzly, wholesome gravy! Thick creams and dips, such as this hummus make my heart beat just as much. They work wonders with simple veggies, and they are a great way to level up a quick and simple roast dinner. This creamy chestnut hummus is filled with earthy flavors inspired by Middle Eastern cuisine with a hint of sweetness from the chestnuts. It's super quick and easy to throw together. All you need is a food processor! It includes a deep flavor from the black garlic, which holds notes of caramel and balsamic and rounds out this creamy dip just beautifully.

Serves 4 to 6

For the Hummus

1 cup (150 g) cooked and peeled chestnuts

1¼ cups (260 g) canned and cooked chickpeas, drained

2 tbsp (32 g) tahini

2 tbsp (30 ml) fresh lemon juice

2 tbsp (4 g) chopped fresh parsley

1 tbsp (15 ml) olive oil

1 tbsp (15 g) minced black garlic

1 tsp fresh rosemary

¼–½ cup (60–125 ml) water

½ tsp sea salt, plus more to taste

¼ tsp ground black pepper, plus more to taste

For Serving

Vegetables or toasted bread, for dipping

Crunchy Rutabaga Fingers (page 128) or Smoky Crusted Green Beans (page 131)

Preheat your oven to 375°F (190°C). Line a baking sheet with parchment paper.

Roast the chestnuts on the baking sheet for 10 minutes, then carefully transfer them to a food processor. Add the chickpeas, tahini, lemon juice, parsley, olive oil, black garlic and rosemary.

Process for 1 to 2 minutes, then add ¼ to ½ cup (60 to 125 ml) of water until you get your desired texture. Season to taste with salt and pepper. Serve the creamy chestnut hummus alongside vegetables or toasted bread. It is also a delicious dip with rutabaga fingers or crusted green beans.

TANGY HARISSA CARROT DIP

With a spicy kick from the harissa paste, this Middle Eastern–inspired carrot dip packs a punch. It will make your tangy dip dreams come true! With a natural sweetness from roasted carrots, this colorful dip has a wonderful zest to counteract the spicy harissa. The addition of a spoonful of dairy-free yogurt brings in some extra creaminess.

Serves 3 to 4

For the Dip

2 lb (1 kg) peeled carrots

1 red onion (roughly 3 oz [85 g])

3 tbsp (45 ml) olive oil, divided

1 tbsp (16 g) harissa paste

2 tbsp (32 g) tomato paste

1 tsp apple cider vinegar

2 tbsp (30 ml) fresh lemon juice

1 tsp ground cumin

¼ tsp sea salt

¼ tsp ground black pepper

½ cup (55 g) roughly chopped walnuts

2 tbsp (30 ml) dairy-free unsweetened yogurt

For Serving

Roasted vegetables

Preheat your oven to 375°F (190°C) and place a rack in the middle. Line a baking sheet with parchment paper.

Chop the carrots roughly into ½-inch (1-cm)-thick sticks. Peel and roughly chop the red onion. Toss both the carrots and the onion in 2 tablespoons (30 ml) of olive oil and transfer them to the baking sheet. Roast them in the middle of the oven for 20 to 25 minutes, or until the onion and carrots are softened.

Transfer them to a food processor and add the harissa paste, tomato paste, apple cider vinegar, lemon juice and remaining olive oil. Process until you get a smooth paste—this should take about 5 minutes. Give your food processor a break in between and carefully scrape down the sides, so the mixture is processed evenly.

Add the cumin, salt and black pepper and pulse until combined. Sprinkle in the walnuts and pulse for six or seven more times to incorporate the nuts. Stir in the dairy-free yogurt and transfer the dip to a serving bowl.

Serve this flavorful dip with roasted vegetables!

GETTING STARTED WITH SEITAN

WHAT IS SEITAN?

Seitan is of Chinese origin and made of gluten, the main protein in wheat. It has been part of Asian cuisines for thousands of years. More people in the Western world have become familiar with it in recent years due to the rising popularity of vegan and vegetarian lifestyles. Seitan is often regarded as a "meat replacement," though I personally find that seitan is its own food category with very unique properties and preparation techniques.

Seitan is simply an amazing discovery in food history. While I love cooking and experimenting with it, I also feel it's important to credit and honor its origin and deep roots in Asian cuisines. I have in no way reinvented the (seitan) wheel with the techniques and ingredients used in this cookbook. After all, seitan has such a rich history, it is very unlikely someone will come up with something completely new and unheard of. But it's a delicious celebration of millions of people who have cooked with seitan before me. I hereby salute you!

HOW IS SEITAN CREATED?

Originally, seitan was created by washing a wheat flour dough to release the soluble starches, leaving you with the non-soluble gluten protein. The resulting gluten dough itself is sticky and elastic, pretty flavor-neutral. It's traditionally cooked before being eaten. Nowadays you can buy vital wheat gluten—which can easily be made into seitan dough by mixing it with liquids.

Some seitan recipes in this book use the flour washing preparation, and others use vital wheat gluten. They are fundamentally different, as they use a different base to create the seitan and result in different shapes and texture. There are pros and cons to both techniques, and a lot of it is down to personal preference. I have picked one technique for each recipe, but feel free to experiment and try other options. Seitan is a fun way to let your creativity run wild in the kitchen!

SEITAN: THE FLOUR WASHING TECHNIQUE (WTF)

On social media this technique is often called WTF: Wash that flour. Here is a breakdown of this technique into easy steps for any scitan-novice.

Wheat flour is made from two main components: starch and protein, gluten being the main protein. Starch dissolves in water, while gluten is non-soluble. When creating seitan from flour, we create a dough ball from flour and water and then wash the dough underwater. The starches dissolve into the water and are washed out of the dough. What is left behind is gluten.

There are slightly different flour washing techniques, depending on the desired end result. The recipes in this book utilize varying times and amounts of flour washing.

When washing a wheat flour dough ball underwater, the water turns white, slightly thick and creamy. Once the water is fully saturated in starches, drain it, add fresh water and continue washing the seitan ball. If you repeat this until the water is almost clear, you have washed out the majority of starches.

The difficulty in creating the perfect washed flour seitan is judging the right time to stop washing the flour. One downside of washing out the majority of wheat starch is that the resulting seitan can often feel a little spongy—not something you would necessarily want, depending on the recipe. If you are not washing out enough starch, the resulting texture can resemble bread.

It needs a little practice to get it right and I have included indications for each WTF recipe. Washing times may vary, if you are using a different flour or wash the flour more/less rigorously, so I'm including this little visual guide for the different washing stages.

Dough ball

Dough ball resting under water

After 1 wash

After 2 washes

Fully washed

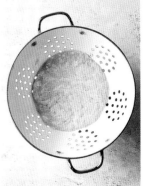
Rinsed and left to drain excess water

How to Cook Washed Flour

There are a couple of options for cooking the washed flour, each of them resulting in a different texture. This is why no two seitan recipes in this book use the exact same technique. Some frequently used options are:

- steaming, which allows for shaping and creates a dense texture
- panfrying, which creates a wonderful crust
- simmering, which allows for additional flavoring and lets the seitan expand in size

These options are often used in combination and followed by roasting to finalize a deliciously succulent and flavorsome seitan.

A Few Simple Tips and Tricks

- When you're making a dough ball, knead it to activate the gluten. Then allow it to rest to fully develop the elasticity of the gluten protein.
- Before washing the dough ball, it should rest underwater for at least 30 minutes. This will help it soften and release the starches. It also makes washing easier.
- During the washing process, don't be alarmed if the gluten dough becomes very loose and almost falls apart. It's normal. After washing, the dough should be placed in a colander, briefly rinsed and then left to drain and rest. If using a fine-mesh sieve, line it with a cheesecloth for easier clean up. During the resting time the gluten strands will come back together and form a firm, uniform dough ball.

 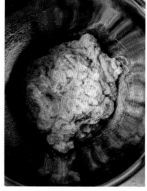

Under-washing   Over-washing

Common Errors When Washing Flour

There are a few common errors that can happen when washing flour.

Under-washing: The water around the dough is white, creamy and saturated with starch. The gluten ball itself is very dense and when you lift it out of the water, you can see white starch bleeding out of it. There is still too much starch in the seitan. Continue washing and refresh the water regularly.

Over-washing: The surrounding water remains almost clear when you have over-washed your dough, and the gluten dough will be extremely loose and often fall apart into individual strands. When cooking over-washed dough, its texture often ends up spongy and elastic. If you've over-washed your dough, add all-purpose flour to your seitan ball.

Not draining the starch water: You need to drain the starchy water frequently during the washing process. If you don't, the seitan will be very slimy on the outside and you're basically creating under-washed dough.

Not rinsing the gluten ball: After the last wash, place the dough ball in a colander and give it a quick rinse to remove excess starches. Not rinsing it can result in a slightly under-washed dough and make it more difficult to handle during the next stage.

Not letting it rest after washing: During the washing process the gluten dough almost falls apart and becomes very light and stringy. After washing, you need to place the dough in a colander, rinse and allow the gluten to rest. During the resting time the gluten develops the texture and it will come back together into a uniform dough ball.

Adding liquid seasoning: While washed dough gives a lot of control over the texture, one downside is that you can't add liquid seasoning. Once washed, the dough is already saturated and repels any additional liquid, so you can only season it with dry ingredients (e.g., spices) or through simmering it in a flavor-filled broth.

Using the wrong type of flour: To create seitan, the base needs to be wheat flour. Any other flour won't work out. It is recommended to use a high-quality high-protein (12% or more) flour. Strong white bread flour is usually a good choice! I personally use a brand called Allinson's that's available from U.K. supermarkets.

SEITAN: VITAL WHEAT GLUTEN (VWG) TECHNIQUE

The alternative—and often quicker technique—to washing flour is using vital wheat gluten, also called VWG. VWG is basically extracted, dried gluten. When combined with liquids, it becomes your gluten dough base for creating seitan.

I find that dough made with VWG is firmer than a washed flour and results in a denser seitan texture. WTF seitan gives a looser, juicier texture. From personal experience, VWG is easier to shape and it's usually my go-to if I want to make a stuffed seitan (e.g., the turkey-style roast in this book on page 67).

To create seitan from VWG, we add dry seasonings to the VWG and combine wet ingredients in a separate bowl. Then we combine and knead everything into a dough ball. As you don't rest and wash the dough multiple times, this is often the quicker method.

Similar to washing flour, you might want to have a little starch in your seitan dough to get a good, non-spongy texture. As VWG is mainly just gluten protein, we need to add a little starch into it to achieve a lovely result. Lots of seitan recipes add chickpea flour to the VWG, but you can also add a little all-purpose flour. You will see this technique all over the VWG recipes in this book.

The cooking methods for VWG are similar to the WTF options and each recipe comes with detailed cooking instructions, so there is no guessing game for you.

SEASONING YOUR SEITAN: WTF VS. VWG

To season WTF seitan, we can add dry herbs and spices into the gluten dough or simmer the seitan in a flavorful broth. Or keep the seitan plain and serve it with a delicious sauce!

To season VWG, it is a little easier to add different flavorings into the seitan. You can use dried seasonings and use liquids in place of water to create a dough. This simple difference (plus differences in texture) is the main reason why some of my recipes in this book use the WTF technique while others use VWG.

I invite you to experiment with both techniques and with different seasonings and preparations. Creating seitan can be an exciting learning curve, and a super delicious journey once you've nailed it!

Seitan on its own doesn't have a strong flavor and takes on seasonings and sauces wonderfully. You might notice an underlying gluteny taste. I don't mind it, but some people are not so keen on it. You can experiment with adding small amounts of vinegar to the liquids of your seitan recipe; this helps neutralize the subtle gluten flavor.

ABOUT THE AUTHOR

Romina Callwitz—better known as Romy—is the food photographer, recipe developer and blogger behind www.romylondonuk.com, where she shares her favorite indulgent vegan recipes with a healthy twist!

Growing up on the Dutch and German borders, Romy found her creative love for photography early and moved to London after finishing her degree in portrait photography. After going vegan in 2014, Romy discovered her passion for getting creative with food and spent more time in the kitchen than anywhere else in the years that followed.

In 2016, she decided it was time to share her creations with the world: She created the blog *Romy London UK* and has since shared her recipes with millions of foodies. She also appeared on *Crazy Delicious*, a Netflix cooking show taking on the challenge of cooking vegan food for Michelin-star renowned chefs. Romy's work has been featured in numerous magazines and publications including *Livekindly*, *Vegan Life* magazine, *Vegan Food & Living*, *Metro*, *Viva!*, *Talkradio*, *Plant Based News*, Channel 4, Netflix, *Distractify*, *Radio Times*, *Reality Titbit*, *Huffington Post*, *Bustle* and many more.

Romy lives just outside of London nowadays, enjoying the British countryside. Besides cooking, photographing and blogging, she enjoys traveling, road trips, gardening and binge-watching true crime series.

ACKNOWLEDGMENTS

When I started sharing my recipes online, my mum always jokingly said "one day I'll find your recipes in a cookbook." Who knew she would be right one day! I never thought this would be possible and never would have been able to get here without the support of my wonderful friends, family—and you, my readers! Honestly, I can't thank you enough!

The biggest THANK-YOU to my Oma Helga, who gave me her creative talent, and Opa Heinz, who taught me to reach for the stars. To my mum and dad, who don't quite understand this whole "vegan thing," but are still accepting and supportive of my "fussiness around food" and every career aspiration I've had over the years. To Schnupen, for being the one that first encouraged me to start sharing my recipes online and for being the best partner in crime I could imagine and never moaning about having to finish my failed experiments along the way. Olaf, Elsa and Sven, for always picking me up when I've had a bad recipe day. My bestie Nicole, for basically being along for the ride and virtually joining me for most of the recipe testing. Sara P., Julia T., Alex M., Lucy W. and Katharine C., for always encouraging me to create more and keeping me sane along the way.

A BIG thank-you to my book publisher, Page Street Publishing, and my editor Caitlin for believing in me and for giving me this platform to share my recipes with the world.

To the numerous creators, bloggers, and chefs that I feel honored to call friends and that inspire me in the kitchen every single day: Samira (@alphafoodie), Rebecca (@thezestylime), Derek Sarno (@wickedhealthy), Jeeca (@thefoodietakesflight) and numerous more. I salute you and am forever grateful to have connected with you.

A special mention also to Lauren Toyota from *Hot for Food,* for inspiring numerous food experiments in my first years of going vegan and opening my eyes to the possibility that letting my creativity run wild in the kitchen is a viable career option.

A big thank-you also to my long-term partners Buy Whole Foods Online, who have supported my recipe creation journey throughout the years and provided lots of the ingredients for my numerous experiments and recipe tests in creating this book. To all the other supportive brands and partners I've worked with throughout the years: One Planet Pizza, Cauldron, Perkier, Oumph!, Squeaky Bean, Veganuary, *Plant Based News*, *Vegan Food & Living* magazine, *Vegan Life* magazine, *PlantBased* magazine, Fry Family, Explore Cuisine and more.

And lastly, to every single wonderful blog reader, newsletter subscriber and follower: You're the best! This book would not exist without you, and I'm eternally grateful for your continued support. I feel honored to create drool-worthy recipes and inspire your vegan kitchen endeavors every single day. Thank you from the bottom of my heart!

INDEX